W9-CUA-299

Statistics on U.S. Immigration

An Assessment of Data Needs for Future Research

Barry Edmonston, Editor

Committee on National Statistics
and
Committee on Population

Commission on Behavioral and Social Sciences and Education

National Research Council

NATIONAL ACADEMY PRESS
Washington, D.C.   1996

NATIONAL ACADEMY PRESS • 2101 Constitution Avenue, NW • Washington, D.C. 20418

NOTICE: The project that is the subject of this report was approved by the Governing Board of the National Research Council, whose members are drawn from the councils of the National Academy of Sciences, the National Academy of Engineering, and the Institute of Medicine. The members of the committee responsible for the report were chosen for their special competences and with regard for appropriate balance.

This report has been reviewed by a group other than the authors according to procedures approved by a Report Review Committee consisting of members of the National Academy of Sciences, the National Academy of Engineering, and the Institute of Medicine.

The National Academy of Sciences is a private, nonprofit, self-perpetuating society of distinguished scholars engaged in scientific and engineering research, dedicated to the furtherance of science and technology and to their use for the general welfare. Upon the authority of the charter granted to it by the Congress in 1863, the Academy has a mandate that requires it to advise the federal government on scientific and technical matters. Dr. Bruce M. Alberts is president of the National Academy of Sciences.

The National Academy of Engineering was established in 1964, under the charter of the National Academy of Sciences, as a parallel organization of outstanding engineers. It is autonomous in its administration and in the selection of its members, sharing with the National Academy of Sciences the responsibility for advising the federal government. The National Academy of Engineering also sponsors engineering programs aimed at meeting national needs, encourages education and research, and recognizes the superior achievements of engineers. Dr. Harold Liebowitz is president of the National Academy of Engineering.

The Institute of Medicine was established in 1970 by the National Academy of Sciences to secure the services of eminent members of appropriate professions in the examination of policy matters pertaining to the health of the public. The Institute acts under the responsibility given to the National Academy of Sciences by its congressional charter to be an adviser to the federal government and, upon its own initiative, to identify issues of medical care, research, and education. Dr. Kenneth I. Shine is president of the Institute of Medicine.

The National Research Council was organized by the National Academy of Sciences in 1916 to associate the broad community of science and technology with the Academy's purposes of furthering knowledge and advising the federal government. Functioning in accordance with general policies determined by the Academy, the Council has become the principal operating agency of both the National Academy of Sciences and the National Academy of Engineering in providing services to the government, the public, and the scientific and engineering communities. The Council is administered jointly by both Academies and the Institute of Medicine. Dr. Bruce M. Alberts and Dr. Harold Liebowitz are chairman and vice chairman, respectively, of the National Research Council.

Funding for this project was provided by the National Institute for Child Health and Human Development and the Immigration and Naturalization Service, and, through their general contributions to the work of the Committee on National Statistics, several other federal agencies.

Library of Congress Catalog Card Number 96-69271

International Standard Book Number 0-309-05275-0

Copyright 1996 by the National Academy of Sciences. All rights reserved.

Additional copies of this report are available from: National Academy Press, 2101 Constitution Avenue, NW, Box 285, Washington, DC 20418

Printed in the United States of America

WITHDRAWN

FEB - 1999

Acknowledgments

Many people contributed time and expertise to the workshop, and the Committee on National Statistics and the Committee on Population appreciate their cooperation and assistance. In particular, Michael Teitelbaum served most ably as chair of the workshop, and he and the workshop participants contributed many thoughts and comments to the shaping of this report. Thanks are due to those who presented papers at the workshop: Barbara Anderson, Frank D. Bean, M. Patricia Fernandez-Kelly, Michael Greenwood, Guillermina Jasso, Douglas Massey, Mark Rosenzweig, Rubén Rumbaut, James P. Smith, Marta Tienda, and Michael White. The papers presented at the workshop served as the starting point for major sections of this report and are noted in the relevant sections. The workshop also benefited from the valuable and stimulating comments of panelists on the papers: Robert Bach, William Butz, Thomas Espenshade, W. Parker Frisbie, Robert Gardner, Sherrie Kossoudji, Alejandro Portes, Brian Roberts, Mary Waters, and Karen Woodrow. Special appreciation is due to those who assisted as rapporteurs: Jeffrey Passel, Lindsay Lowell, Lisa Roney, Steve Sandell, and Robert Warren.

Workshop participants realized the importance of having an ongoing discussion of changing demands for immigration statistics and especially the ways in which federal agencies attempt to respond to those data needs. One outcome of the workshop was the formation of the Interagency Taskforce on Immigration, at which representatives of federal agencies with an interest in immigration have met regularly since December 1992 under the sponsorship of the Immigration and Naturalization Service (INS). Robert Warren, research coordinator of the

INS Office of Policy and Planning, has chaired the task force.[1] The task force has formed a number of working groups that are developing ideas and programs to improve immigration statistics in a variety of ways, including data on temporary migrants, data from longitudinal surveys, immigration data in the Current Population Survey, and increased exploitation of administrative data.

The agenda for the workshop was developed in consultation with Edward Lynch and Robert Warren from the Immigration and Naturalization Service, Nancy Moss and Jeffery Evans from the National Institute of Child Health and Human Development, Miron Straf from the Committee on National Statistics, and Linda Martin from the Committee on Population (now at the Rand Corp.). John Haaga from the Committee on Population assisted with the final report.

Barry Edmonston from the Committee on National Statistics was responsible for the conduct of the workshop as well as the preparation of the report. The task of coordinating the workshop was accomplished by Michele Conrad, also from the Committee on National Statistics, who helped to ready the report for publication. The report benefited from the thoughtful comments of reviewers and the editorial skills of Christine McShane of the Commission on Behavioral and Social Sciences and Education.

We would also like to acknowledge former members of both committees who served during the time the workshop was developed and convened. Such members of the Committee on National Statistics include Burton H. Singer (former chair), Martin H. David, Noreen Goldman, Louis Gordon, and Dorothy P. Rice. Former members of the Committee on Population include Samuel T. Preston (former chair), T. Paul Schultz, Susan C. M. Scrimshaw, Barbara Boyle Torrey, and James Trussell. The input of these former members of both committees greatly helped shape the development of the workshop.

[1] At the time of the workshop, Warren was director of the INS Statistics Division. Linda Gordon is currently acting director of the Statistics Division.

Contents

Statistics on U.S. Immigration

An Assessment of Data Needs for Future Research

Summary

In September 1992, the Committee on National Statistics and the Committee on Population of the National Research Council held a workshop to explore data collection and data preparation on immigration in the United States. One purpose was to assist the Immigration and Naturalization Service in developing a statistical information system, as required by the Immigration Act of 1990. The other purpose was to suggest possible improvements to the data collection and analysis efforts of federal statistical agencies and the social science research community. Using as a basis the presentations and discussions that took place, the committees make the following conclusions and recommendations.

CONCLUSIONS

Research Issues

The committees' conclusions regarding research issues cover four areas:

• It is extremely important to examine immigrants by nationality groups, yet the overall sample size of available surveys limits the ability to conduct analysis of immigrants by countries of origin. The need for large-scale data sets—possibly including new longitudinal surveys—on immigrants is a challenge for immigration research.

• Many surveys and the decennial census have limited information for distinguishing immigrant origins. Some surveys include virtually no data on immigrant status (whether a person is a naturalized citizen, a legal immigrant, a refugee, or a foreign-born person in some other visa status), whereas other surveys (and the census) provide information only on foreign-born persons—yielding limited data, for example, on the children of the foreign-born.[1] At a time when U.S. immigration is both substantial and diverse, research is hampered by the inability to use existing data for immigration studies.

• The experiences of immigrants in the United States vary enormously and affect people's adjustment to life in this country. Studies of the use of welfare programs—to mention one important policy topic—need to distinguish among illegal aliens, legal immigrants, and refugees for analysis. Unfortunately, information on legal status and the visa status (for legal aliens) is absent from most available data.

• Of all the areas that require more research and improved data, no topic requires more systematic attention than family and social networks. The family is an important factor before, during, and after immigration. And "after" extends a long time: the status of the family greatly affects the children of immigrants. Several data sets, including the records of the Immigration and Naturalization Service, could benefit from improvements in the study of the immigrant family.

Research Improvements

Having noted the priority policy questions for immigration data (see the section on establishing data priorities in Chapter 1), the committees also draw conclusions regarding broad areas for improvement in Immigration and Naturalization Service records:

• Cooperative efforts are needed to improve immigration statistics. The matching of administrative records, especially records on program and welfare use, offers many possibilities for improved immigration data. It would be useful to match welfare records to a sample of recent immigrants, for example, to make comparisons with the native-born. The results of such an effort would be beneficial for both the study of immigration and social program use.

• Coordination between the Immigration and Naturalization Service and the Social Security Administration could provide improved data and should be encouraged. Matching records from the two agencies could provide longitudinal data on earnings for immigrants, an important but neglected topic of policy study. One possibility for exploration would be to assign a social security number to immigrants as part of the Immigration and Naturalization Service's administra-

---

[1]The 1980 and 1990 censuses did not collect data on the nativity of the respondent's parents. Census data on the children of the foreign-born exist only for children who reside in the household with their parents. For children of immigrants who do not live with their parents, census data do not provide information about such important topics as the education, employment, and income of this transitional generation.

tive procedures. A second possibility would be to take a sample of records on entering immigrants from past periods and link them to the Social Security Administration's records to provide data on earnings since arrival in the United States. With Immigration and Naturalization Service data linked to earnings information on individuals, dependents, and relatives, meaningful information on family processes would also be available for study.

• Conducting sample surveys of immigrants, using Immigration and Naturalization Service or other records, would add valuable information about newly arriving immigrants. There are special problems in surveying immigrants because they are widely dispersed in the U.S. population and are few in number in many areas. One possible survey design would be to use a sample of approved applications for a permanent resident visa—known as a green card. A relatively accurate address is provided by green card applicants. It would be possible to obtain information by enclosing a mail questionnaire, perhaps using several different languages, when the green card is delivered.

RECOMMENDATIONS

The committees make two kinds of recommendations: (1) on additional sources for the data needed for program and research purposes and (2) on new questions and refinements of questions within existing data sources in order to improve the understanding of immigration and immigrant trends.

Parental Nativity

A question on parental nativity (place of birth of respondents' parents) is an important one for the decennial census. Although such information was collected on the 1970 and earlier censuses, it was not included on either the 1980 or the 1990 census. Parental nativity data provide the information required to examine the social and economic characteristics of the sons and daughters of immigrants. Children of immigrants are a critical generation for study: they reflect the success and rapidity of adjustment of immigrants to U.S. society. The children of immigrants are a pivotal, young subgroup of a national population increasingly affected by large-scale immigration. Census questions require a strong political mandate for inclusion; for the 1990 census, there was no adequate mandate for including parental nativity on the questionnaire. The Immigration Act of 1990 now provides a federal mandate for parental nativity information.

Recommendation 1. We urge that the Immigration and Naturalization Service work with other federal agencies and the Bureau of the Census, under the overall direction of the Office of Management and Budget, to include key immigration questions on future censuses, in-

cluding a question on nativity and parental nativity, based on the requirements of the Immigration Act of 1990.

Public Use Microdata Sample

An important source of decennial data for immigration research is the Public Use Microdata Sample (PUMS). The Bureau of the Census's 1990 PUMS files are 1 and 5 percent samples of the individual data from the decennial census. All individual identifications, including specific geographic residence, are deleted from the PUMS files in order to preserve individual privacy. The PUMS files are widely used by immigration researchers, particularly for the study of numerically small and widely scattered racial and ethnic groups. One valuable enhancement of the PUMS files would be to add such contextual data as local unemployment rates—the study of the impact of immigration on employment levels requires local-area data.

Recommendation 2. We recommend that the Bureau of the Census consider ways to add local-area contextual data to the Public Use Microdata Sample (PUMS) files. Contextual data on such variables as local employment, income, education, and racial and ethnic composition would measurably improve this important data set for academic and policy research on immigrants.

Current Population Survey

The Current Population Survey, which produces a great deal of valuable data, is the key federal survey available for immigration analysis. For more than a decade prior to 1991, the Current Population Survey occasionally included questions on parental nativity and other immigration-related issues. Parental nativity—and such related questions as citizenship and year of immigration—are essential for immigration research and should be included as key questions as a regular part of the Current Population Survey.

Subsequent to the September 1992 workshop, and partially in response to discussions at the workshop, a group of federal agencies worked to place a nativity question on the Current Population Survey. As of 1994, the Current Population Survey collects nativity information for household members and parents of members, allowing researchers to distinguish among foreign-born, native-born of foreign-born parents, and native-born of native-born parents. In addition, the survey includes data on the year of entry for immigrants and citizenship status. The survey makes available basic information on immigration for all survey months and for all members of the household. It is notable that these data are available as well for all supplements to the Current Population Survey.

Recommendation 3. **The committees applaud the introduction of key questions on nativity as a regular part of the Current Population Survey.** **Questions on nativity, parental nativity, citizenship, and year of entry into the United States provide information essential to the understanding of immigration in this country.** **We urge the Bureau of the Census to retain these key immigration-related topics on the Current Population Survey.**

Recommendation 4. **We recommend that the Bureau of the Census, in consultation with federal agencies and immigration researchers, review the possibility of adding special immigration questions to the Current Population Survey.** **Additional, more detailed immigration-related questions would enhance the value of the Current Population Survey data for immigration policy research.** **Such questions might be included on the Current Population Survey on a special basis, perhaps on one of the special monthly supplements, or on a periodic basis, depending on the purpose and usefulness of the data.**

Joint Mexico-United States Surveys

Whereas the Current Population Survey is the key survey for use by immigration researchers, there have been discussions in recent decades about a joint survey in Mexico and the United States for immigration study. Such surveys would have value for policy studies in both countries. They could explore potential immigration, immigration before departure and after arrival, and return migrants. Joint surveys have been discussed before in general terms; there may be a real opportunity for them at this time.

Recommendation 5. **We recommend that U.S. federal statistical agencies meet with their counterpart institutions in Mexico to discuss the potential for establishing joint surveys on immigration.** **Such a meeting should include key immigration researchers from both countries.**

Immigration and Naturalization Service Records

Some valuable changes have occurred in the past decade at the Immigration and Naturalization Service. Some were made in part to respond to an earlier National Research Council report (Levine et al., 1985). One suggestion that emerged from the 1992 workshop has been implemented: the Immigration and Naturalization Service has convened a group that meets regularly to coordinate improvements in federal immigration data.

Despite the changes made in immigration data since 1985—for the Immigration and Naturalization Service and other agencies collecting immigration data—

weaknesses in the data persist: the Current Population Survey questions on nativity have not been asked regularly, data on emigration and illegal aliens remain poor, little is known about foreign students and new citizens, and procedures have not been developed to ensure continued adequate analysis and dissemination of immigration information. Some obvious opportunities for improving immigration data remain. Examples include establishing an advisory committee to advise the associate commissioner and the Statistics Division and conducting a review of all federal agencies that gather immigration data or for which immigration data have a substantial impact (e.g., educational planning).

Workshop participants made suggestions for the Immigration and Naturalization Service to explore the collection of new data, including improving data on nonimmigrants, adding information on immigrant adjustment to information on previous nonimmigrant status, matching administrative records, conducting a longitudinal survey of immigrants, doing special surveys, and sponsoring case studies. Survey data on new immigrants would offer useful additional data for immigration policy research.

> **Recommendation 6. We recommend that the Immigration and Naturalization Service establish the design and usefulness of a survey of green card applicants. A survey of new immigrants appears to be feasible, using the relatively accurate addresses that are provided by immigrants in order to receive their permanent resident visa.**

A survey of new immigrants would provide cross-sectional data on legal new entrants into the United States. An ongoing survey, perhaps conducted annually or every few years, would also provide baseline data for longitudinal data collection. The workshop did not include discussion of specific proposals for such longitudinal data collection, although future study could weigh the merits and design for such a proposal.

A Longitudinal Survey

The National Institute for Child Health and Human Development, one of the sponsors of the workshop, requested that the workshop participants address the potential value of a longitudinal survey of immigrants, a type of survey that has been suggested as important for the advancement of immigration research. Participants reviewed several types of data collection for longitudinal data, spending the most time discussing the merits of a prospective sample (a survey of immigrants who are then followed over time). The purpose of the workshop discussion was to understand the value and limitations of such a survey; it was not to propose a specific survey design or to endorse the need for a longitudinal survey. Chapter 7 summarizes the discussion on the value of a longitudinal survey of immigrants, alternatives to a new survey, and some technical issues in survey design.

1

Introduction

During the 1980s, the United States received about 8 million immigrants, approximately 800,000 per year, including both legal admissions and illegal entrants who later received amnesty and legal residence. The volume has increased in the 1990s, with about 900,000 immigrants arriving each year. Furthermore, over the past 30 years, the source countries of these immigrants to the United States have shifted dramatically, from primarily European countries in the 1950s to primarily Asian and Latin American countries in the 1990s. Now is a good time to take stock of immigration statistics—which indicate the number, relative size, and characteristics of immigrant populations, as well as how they fare after entry into the United States.

INTEREST IN IMMIGRATION ISSUES

Long-standing interest in immigration issues and in improving data related to immigration in the United States is shared by the National Research Council, specifically the Committee on National Statistics and the Committee on Population; several federal agencies, including the Immigration and Naturalization Service, the National Institute of Child Health and Human Development, and the Bureau of the Census; and the social science research community involved in immigration studies. This confluence of interest led to a request in 1992 from the Immigration and Naturalization Service and the National Institute on Child Health and Human Development to the National Research Council committees to conduct a workshop on U.S. immigration statistics.

Previous assessments of immigration statistics have been made by several researchers. Hutchinson (1958) reviewed statistics on international migration to the United States, noting the slow pace of improvement. Tomasi and Keely's (1975) volume on international migration includes useful discussion of U.S. data issues. Kraly (1979) provides an excellent review of the various sources of immigration data and their limitations. This report emphasizes an assessment of current immigration data; the assessments noted above provide useful reviews of historical immigration data, as well as topics of international migration not discussed in detail here (i.e., emigration data).

An earlier National Research Council report, by a panel of the Committee on National Statistics (Levine et al., 1985), made a number of important recommendations for improving data for the study of immigration. In particular, the panel recommended that the commissioner of the Immigration and Naturalization Service:

• Issue an explicit statement stating that the collection, cumulation, and tabulation of reliable, accurate, and timely statistical information on immigration is a basic responsibility and inherent mission of the Immigration and Naturalization Service;

• Establish a Division of Immigration Statistics, reporting directly to an associate commissioner or an equivalent level;

• Direct and implement the recruitment of a full complement of competent, trained professionals with statistical capabilities and subject-area expertise;

• Establish an advisory committee of experts in the use and production of immigration-related data, to advise the associate commissioner and the proposed Division of Immigration Statistics about needs for new or different types of data, to review existing data and data collection methodology, and to provide the Immigration and Naturalization Service with independent evaluation of its statistical products, plans, and performance;

• Establish formal liaison with other federal and state agencies involved in the collection and analysis of immigration- and emigration-related data; and

• Initiate a review of all data-gathering activities to eliminate duplication, minimize burden and waste, review specific data needs and uses, improve question wording and format design, standardize definitions and concepts, document methodologies, introduce statistical standards and procedures, and promote efficiencies in the use of staff and resources.

Several subsequent legislative mandates relied on recommendations contained in the 1985 report, including the one for the establishment of a Statistics Division at the Immigration and Naturalization Service.

With the 1985 report as a point of departure, participants in the workshop were asked to first assess the needs for data collection on immigration and immigrant adjustment.[1] This task was intended to help the Immigration and Naturalization Service meet its mandate to assess the impact of immigration on the U.S. population; it was also intended to aid the National Institute of Child Health and Human Development in assessing the data needs of the research community. In particular, that agency asked that a portion of the workshop discussion be devoted to consideration of a longitudinal survey of immigrants, a type of survey that some researchers have advocated in recent years. A second task was to discuss the agenda for immigration research and to consider priorities for future data. In planning the workshop, the committees hoped to highlight the important topic of immigration policy and research.

SHIFTS IN IMMIGRATION PATTERNS

The age of mass migration to the United States is not over. In the 30 years since the United States discarded nationality quotas in 1965, 14 to 15 million immigrants have been legally admitted—and the numbers are growing. An annual average of 450,000 immigrants were admitted in the 1970s, almost 800,000 in the 1980s (taking both legal and illegal immigrants into account), and about 700,000 in 1992.

None of these figures includes the more than 3 million applicants for legalization from illegal aliens under the 1986 Immigration Reform and Control Act (IRCA). The 1986 IRCA legislation offered amnesty (through a general legalization and a program for special agricultural workers) to illegal aliens who were residing in the United States. The legislation also contained a number of provisions aimed at reducing illegal immigration, including an increase in Border Patrol activities. The effect of IRCA immigrants on the immigration figures began to be felt in fiscal 1989 and continued through the early 1990s. In fiscal 1991, for example, the Immigration and Naturalization Service reported the admission of more than 700,000 legal immigrants and over 1,100,000 legalizations through the 1986 act (U.S. Immigration and Naturalization Service, 1992:20). The figures quoted above also do not reflect the provisions of the Immigration Act of 1990, which increased authorized immigration, especially for business and job-related visa categories, beginning in 1992.

The Immigration Act of 1965 changed the primary focus of the criteria for admission from nationality to family reunification, with a smaller emphasis on needed skills. This focus on family contributed substantially to the increase in admissions. The 1990 act established a "pierceable cap" on family-sponsored

---

[1]Immigrant adjustment is assumed to involve a variety of social, political, and economic changes, taking the local context into account. For example, the adjustment of an immigrant in a Spanish-speaking section of Miami would differ from that of the same immigrant living in an English-speaking suburb of Minneapolis.

immigrants at 520,000 annually, and also increased the number of occupationally related visas from 58,000 to 155,000. At the same time, the principle of family reunification operated as well for the skill-oriented categories: of 116,000 skilled-oriented immigrant visas awarded in fiscal 1992, only about 60,000 went to skilled principals; the balance went to spouses and dependent children. Finally, there has been an additional source of increased immigration: refugees, particularly from Cuba and Southeast Asia, have added large numbers to the total admissions during the past 25 years. About 870,000 of a total of 2,100,000 refugees, entered the United States from these areas between 1961 and 1993.

Immigration Today

Not only has the size of immigration cohorts changed; so have their national origins. Prior to 1965, arrivals from many countries in Europe dominated immigration flows to the United States. For the early decades of this century, Asians were excluded from entering the United States as immigrants. As late as the 1950s, Europeans (including immigrants from Canada, Australia, and New Zealand) represented 53 percent of immigrant flows to the United States. At that time, Latin American and Caribbean immigrants accounted for 25 percent and Asians for only 6 percent of admissions. In the 1980s, Asians made up 43 percent of admissions, Latin Americans and Caribbeans 40 percent, and Europeans only 11 percent.

Perceptions of the Past

America has honored its immigrant tradition, paying homage to a "golden age of immigration" at the turn of the century. In 1992, the doors of the immigration buildings on Ellis Island in New York City were once again opened, this time as a museum in memory of the millions of immigrants who first entered the United States through that port. The perception of past immigration has a patina of nostalgia about immigrants, ethnic neighborhoods, and hard-working parents who encouraged their children's education, leading to social mobility. As these images are being enshrined, however, some observers point out the conditions of past immigrants as chronicled and photographed by Jacob Riis and others of his time, whose photographs showed the poverty and hardship of immigrant life.

It is also important to remember that the dominant view at the turn of the century was that social problems were caused by the existence of immigrant-based ethnic ghettos. Fears about the impact of foreigners on the "American way of life" led to adoption of the national origin quota system of the 1920s, which was revised by the Immigration and Nationality Act of 1952 (it still based national origin quotas on the 1920 census but set a minimum of 100 and a maximum of 2,000 each for Asian countries) and was finally abolished by the Immigration and Nationality Act Amendments of 1965. A shift in the perception of a romanticized past period of immigration to the social problems of current immigration has affected the public's judgment about the desirability of large-scale immigration. Perceptions do not always accurately reflect the contributions of immigration to national well-being, or to the problems that are attributed to it. Much of the current debate about mass immigration involves public perceptions more than social facts.

Effects of Immigration

As a result of declining U.S. fertility and the increase in legal immigrant and refugee entries, legal immigration now accounts for a substantial number of new additions to the population. However, immigrants are not evenly distributed across the country. Some regions, states, counties, and cities are very heavily affected by immigration, and with quite differing results. In each area, the effects seem to be functions of the general condition of the economy and society, the number and tempo of immigrant admissions, immigrant characteristics (refugee status, education and occupational skill level, culture, and other factors related to employment and adaptability), and the immigrant-receiving traditions of the community.

Because immigration varies in volume and type by communities and regions, it requires detailed study in order to disentangle the various impacts. Detailed local and specific studies, as well as overall studies of immigration to the United States, are needed. The impact of immigration is more important for some communities than for others. For example, San Diego and Los Angeles counties are currently weighing the cost of immigrants, with the implicit conclusion that immigration is affecting those communities adversely to a larger degree than other communities.

ESTABLISHING DATA PRIORITIES

The purpose of the workshop was to assess and identify needs for immigration data to answer two fundamental questions: (1) How are immigrants adjusting? (2) What effects are immigrants having on U.S. society? Immigration policy issues involve four key areas of inquiry:

1. the characteristics of immigrant-sending countries,
2. the characteristics of the United States as an immigrant-receiving country,
3. characteristics of immigrants themselves, and
4. the social and economic effects of immigration.

These four areas illuminate the important immigration policy issues that provide an organizing framework for the assessment of priorities for data needs presented in this report.

The number and characteristics of immigrants entering the United States are affected not only by U.S. immigration policy, but also by other factors in the United States and in the sending countries. Job opportunities, educational aspirations, the presence of suitable ethnic communities, and family ties affect the decision to migrate. Factors in the sending country, such as political or social unrest, may also influence migration decisions.

The proximity of sending countries and the ease of movement to the United States are also factors, along with language and cultural similarities. Immigrant characteristics are also influenced by the ability to afford to emigrate to the United States, familiarity with U.S. society, and perceptions about success in adapting to a new country.

Characteristics of the United States and the sending countries also influence the adjustment of immigrants after arrival. The receptivity of the local community, ethnic and family supports, job and school opportunities, health and social service availability all influence the adjustment of immigrants. Immigrant behavior may also be influenced by family and friendship ties to the country of origin and by economic, social, and political events there. Such events may lead immigrants to send money back; conversely, opportunities in the United States may lead immigrants to borrow money from family or friends in the country of origin.

Immigrant characteristics and behavior have effects on U.S. society. The flow of immigrants into and out of the United States occurs through a variety of pathways, both legal and illegal, and together with their characteristics defines the impact of immigrants at one point in time. Among the most important characteristics for study are the country of origin (including language and cultural heritage), age at entry, reason for migrating, legal status, occupational and education skills, English language proficiency, and social and economic resources.

Both immigrant characteristics and country characteristics (the country of origin as well as the local community of U.S. settlement) have a major influence on the adjustment of immigrants and their children—a "generational" adjustment. We include consideration of the offspring of immigrants in this report in order to stress the need for a long-term view of the social impact of immigration. Immigrants themselves affect society only during their lifetimes, but subsequent generations make a more lasting impact.

Immigrant adjustment includes changes in individual behavior, such as cultural patterns (English language use and ability, religion, food preferences), social and economic achievements (labor force participation, job skills, education, income), family status (number of children, intermarriage), health and social well-being, cultural and political values, and participation in social and political organizations. The behavior can vary widely among immigrants and can differ markedly among individuals as they adjust to a new society.

The policy questions that frame the workshop discussion span six broad topic areas: demographic change, families and households, labor markets, public services, institutions, and culture.

• Demographic change: Immigrants and their offspring increase the population of the United States and affect its composition (e.g., age, sex, racial and ethnic distribution) and geographic distribution. These demographic changes can have short- and long-term implications for U.S. society.

Major policy questions include: (1) What is the impact of immigration on the absolute and relative levels of population growth? (2) What is the effect of immigration on the age and sex distribution of the population? (3) What is the influence of immigration on the racial and ethnic composition of the population? (4) What is the impact of immigration on the geographic distribution of the population?

• Families and households: Immigrants vary in their family composition and household structure, which may provide additional support for their adjustment or capacity to provide needed social and economic resources. Immigrant families are important influences on subsequent marriage and childbearing, care of the elderly, remittances, the use of public services, and educational achievement.

Major policy questions include: (1) How does immigration affect the family and household structure of immigrants? (2) How do family networks affect subsequent immigration (through the family reunification provisions of U.S. immigration visas or through the encouragement of immigration through other legal or illegal entry)? (3) How does immigration affect subsequent marriage and childbearing, including the behavior of immigrant children? (4) How does immigration affect variables of particular importance for the family, including the health of immigrants and their family members, care for the elderly, labor force involvement, remittances, public assistance, and education?

• Labor markets: Labor market outcomes of immigration are frequently discussed in current public policy debates. Some fear that immigrants, particularly illegal immigrants, depress wages and take jobs that would otherwise be filled by native-born workers. Others point to the beneficial impact of immigrant workers on the U.S. labor market through the creation of additional jobs, the infusion of capital, and the increased ability of U.S. businesses to compete internationally.

Important policy questions include: (1) How well do immigrants perform in the U.S. economy? (2) What characteristics of immigrants indicate those who adapt most successfully and can make a contribution to economic growth? (3) What impact do immigrants have on the earnings and employment opportunities of native-born citizens? (4) Are there native-born workers who are negatively affected and others who are positively affected by immigration?

• Public services: Immigrants pay taxes and contribute to social insurance funds such as state unemployment and national social security; in turn, they draw on public social services if they are eligible. The extent of these contributions and demands has an impact on the larger society through shifts in the distribution of the tax burden throughout the population; they also may have differential effects on local and state governments. In addition, the public services delivered to immigrants may play a part in modifying the effects they have on other social outcomes: for example, English language improvement programs may increase their general job skills and income, with ultimate impacts on tax revenues and the economy.

Major policy questions include: (1) What are the public service costs of providing services to immigrant populations relative to their tax contributions? (2) To what extent are the public service needs of immigrants being met? (3) How do public services contribute to the rate of change in the conditions and behavior of immigrants?

• Institutions: The extent to which immigrants are accepted by and participate in the formal and informal institutions and organizations of the United States may effect institutional changes. Immigrant participation in U.S. institutions and organizations is a major indication of assimilation, although their participation often influences the nature, outlook, and activities of institutions. Intragroup hostility or competition are potential problems when new immigrants resist institutional assimilation through the creation and maintenance of separate institutions, and when native-born residents and older immigrants resist the participation of new immigrants in institutions.

Major policy questions include: (1) To what extent do immigrant populations create and maintain "separate" economic, social, and political institutions? (2) How do institutions respond to immigrant populations, especially in schools, churches, and legal systems? (3) How are the characteristics of public institutions related to participation by and tolerance for immigrant populations?

• Culture: When two different cultures come together, each affects the other. Some researchers have referred to a cultural melting pot when these reciprocal influences are complete, with no remaining differences in cultural patterns between the original groups. Or cultural influences may be partial, with some patterns shaved and others retained, creating a cultural mosaic. Culture in the United States has been shaped by many past immigrants, and new immigrants continue to have an impact, both regionally and nationally, resulting in changes in consumption patterns, customs and religious practices, art, and even language. Historically, immigrants, and especially their children, have conformed over time to American culture in such a way that, even though their culture of origin may have an impact on the larger society, American culture has not become unduly segmented. How new waves of immigrants adjust to American culture and the degree to which Americans embrace new cultural diversity will affect the extent to which American culture becomes more diverse or more homogeneous.

Major policy questions include: (1) To what extent and how quickly do immigrant populations conform to American culture? (2) To what extent do immigrant populations influence American culture? (3) How much do native-born Americans resist the cultural influences of immigrant groups?

ADEQUACY OF IMMIGRATION DATA

Although data sources are available for studying many issues related to the broad features of current immigration, many of them focus either on all immigrants or on only one or a small number of immigrant groups. Some survey samples include so few foreign-born people that analysis cannot be performed for specific nationality groups. Other data sets are limited to immigrants from one country or from a single region, making comparative studies impossible. Many federal data sources were not designed to study the new immigration flows. Given these circumstances, the workshop held by the two committees represents a major effort to examine current data collection and analysis on immigration; the committees' recommendations about the needed broad, long-term changes in immigration statistics stem from that examination.

Immigration affects a wide variety of social and economic institutions—schools, labor markets, population growth and distribution, and consumer products, to name a few. Data are needed in order to understand better the impact that immigration has on society. For example, in studying the mortality rates of blacks, Samuel Preston noted at the workshop that a critical weakness is the poor quality of immigration data. Such mortality studies require good data by age and sex, including information on immigration by age and sex.

DEFINITION OF TERMS

A number of terms are used in this report with specific meaning. At the outset, it is useful to distinguish between *immigration* and *immigrants*. Most of the federal government's statistics on immigration pertain to the process of applying for entry into the United States and information collected at the time of entry. Once a person has entered the United States—and becomes an immigrant—there are relatively few data sets that capture the immigrant's experiences. The Immigration and Naturalization Service collects data on immigrants if they apply for naturalization, for example. But because typically a naturalization application cannot be made until five years after entrance into the United States, it has virtually no information on immigrants in the crucial years immediately after their arrival.

The processes of movement are described as *immigration* and *emigration*. We refer to immigrants as foreign-born people legally moving to the United States and emigrants as U.S. residents who depart to some other country. The use of terms for international migration varies with the country perspective: Mexican immigrants in the United States would be viewed by Mexico as emigrants to the

United States. This report refers to immigrants and emigrants from the point of view of the United States.

The total number of arrivals of immigrants and the departures of emigrants is called *gross migration*, or the *volume of migration*. *Net migration* is the difference between the total arrivals and the total departures.

When large groups of individuals or families migrate together, *collective migration* occurs. If migration is not in a concerted form, the migration is referred to as *individual migration*. When the number of migrants is large, it is called *mass migration*.

We use the term *immigrant* to refer to a foreign-born person who has established residence in the United States. In speaking of foreign-born people, we make no distinction about their legal status—they may be legal residents, refugees, or undocumented migrants. This use of the term *immigrant* corresponds to the foreign-born population enumerated in the census. We refer to *legal immigrant* to indicate that the immigrant is a lawful resident of the United States.

A *refugee* is usually someone who migrates to the United States as a result of strong pressures to move because continued stay in the country of origin may expose him or her to dangers to life or well-being. In the United States, refugees are on temporary residence status at the time of admission but are eligible for permanent residence after one year. (Refugees are under a special status for their first year; they are not immigrants with permanent lawful residency and are, therefore, treated as "nonimmigrants".)

The process by which immigrants adjust themselves to conditions in the United States is divided into three categories: (1) *naturalization*, the acquisition of legal citizenship; (2) *assimilation*, integration into the social structure on terms of equality; and (3) *acculturation*, the process of relinquishing the customs and values of the country of origin and adopting the broad values of American society. In a society as heterogeneous as the United States, such values cannot be narrowly defined nor characterized as uniform.

We use the term *illegal alien* or *illegal immigrant* to refer to a foreign-born person who resides in the United States illegally. Illegal aliens are often described as if they are a homogeneous group. This confuses debate and makes it difficult to consider the ways in which individuals enter into and depart from the illegal alien population. People become illegal aliens in the United States in three primary ways: (1) by illegal entry into the country, (2) by legal entry but staying beyond the authorization period, and (3) by legal entry but violating the terms of entry. Illegal entry into the United States occurs when an individual enters without inspection, usually by crossing the land border into the United States other than through a lawful port of entry. Many people enter by this route from Mexico, and it is a prominent route for those who reside in Mexico but work in the United States.

Analysis of illegal entry into the United States is complicated by the use of border-crossing cards that are issued by the United States to Mexican residents.

Border-crossing cards are usually issued to residents of Mexican border communities who have steady work in Mexico and allow the bearer to visit a limited geographic range inside the United States for up to 72 hours. The cards are intended for routine shopping and visiting; some, however, use the cards to cross into the United States to work. Others who have border-crossing cards enter the United States illegally in order to avoid the lines at the lawful port of entry.

Students can become illegal aliens by overstaying the authorization period of their visa or by working beyond the limits authorized by the student visa. They may enter the United States legally but then continue to reside and work there illegally.

Individuals who enter the United States on a tourist visa but then become illegally employed are the most common example of the third type of illegal alien—those violating the terms of entry.

This report does not discuss various groups of foreign-born people who reside temporarily in the United States with nonimmigrant visas. These categories of people include foreign students, diplomats, and some representatives of international organizations. The workshop discussion, as reflected in this report, centered on legal and illegal immigrant flows for groups with long-term U.S. residence.

ORGANIZATION OF THE REPORT

This report summarizes the key points of the workshop discussions, which are the basis for the committees' recommendations. The volume does not include the workshop papers, nor does it offer a detailed survey of the research literature. Citations are given, however, to surveys of the theoretical and empirical literature.

The first four chapters that follow this introduction summarize the workshop discussion of immigration data needs in four areas of study: immigration trends, the effects of immigration and assimilation, labor force issues, and family and social networks. They include discussion of major research challenges, including topics for further study. Chapter 6 is an overview of the key data needs for immigration research, classified by type of data. Chapter 7 is a discussion of the value of longitudinal studies of immigration. The appendix includes the workshop agenda and participants and a list of the papers presented.

2

Trends in U.S. Immigration

This chapter summarizes the workshop session that provided details on the characteristics and magnitude of trends in U.S. immigration.

A DEMOGRAPHIC PERSPECTIVE[1]

Trends Since 1900

The workshop discussion of demographic trends in immigration began with trends in the average number of immigrants (Figure 1). The annual numbers of new entrants reached their highest volume during the first two decades of this century. As a result of the passage of the National Origins Quota Act in 1924, the Great Depression of the 1930s, and an unfavorable immigration climate during World War II, immigration dropped to one-tenth of the record-setting levels during the next 25 years. Specifically, the number of entrants decreased from over 700,000 per year during the first 20 years of the century to less than 70,000 per year from 1925 to 1945 (Bean, 1992:4). After this lull and continuing for the 50 years since 1945, legal immigration has been moving steadily upward, reaching levels by the late 1980s and early 1990s similar to the all-time highs set in the early part of this century. And if the legalizations of previously illegal aliens resulting from the 1986 Immigration Reform and Control Act (IRCA) are included in the totals, the recent levels exceed all previous highs.

---

[1]This section draws on the paper presented at the workshop by Frank D. Bean.

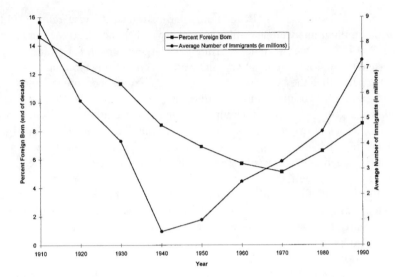

FIGURE 1 Average number of immigrants and percentage foreign-born of U.S. population, by decade, 1910-1990.

The major features of post-World War II immigration include: (1) increasing numbers of illegal aliens entering the United States, (2) increasing numbers of refugees and those seeking asylum, (3) substantially increasing numbers of immigrants from Third World countries (mostly from Asia and Latin America) and concomitant declines in the fraction of immigrants of European origin, (4) increasing proportions of immigrants admitted on the basis of occupational and skills criteria rather than national origin or family connection criteria, and (5) enormously increasing numbers of people admitted for short periods of time on so-called nonimmigrant visas (students, tourists, and business travelers). This last phenomenon is not technically considered to be immigration, but it nonetheless carries considerable consequences for immigration. It often is a prelude to subsequent entry, and its facilitation by the Immigration Act of 1990 is viewed by many observers as a compromise in the face of proposals to allow even higher levels of business-related immigration than were actually written into the legislation.

In the mid-1970s, growth in real wages began to level off, unemployment rose as the country experienced a recession, and calls for immigration reform began to emerge (Bean et al., 1987). Frequently these consisted of restrictionist outcries against the new immigration, often stated in the form of unsubstantiated claims about the pernicious nature of immigration and its harmful effects on the country. During the 1980s, a body of social science research emerged that found little basis for the claims that immigration was generating substantial negative economic and social effects (Bean et al., 1988). In fact, the research tended to show that immigrants were assimilating socially and economically within a reasonable period of time, were not exerting very large labor market effects on the wages and unemployment of natives, and were not consuming more in the way of public benefits than they were paying in taxes. To be sure, because the composition of immigrant origins was changing, questions were being raised about whether the skill levels of immigrants were actually declining, both within and across countries of origin (Borjas, 1990). The general conclusion that emerged from the research on this period was that immigration did not appear to be generating much in the way of large effects, either positive or negative (for a recent discussion, see Espenshade, 1994).

Almost all of the research cited above, however, has been based on data collected during the 1970s or, in one or two instances, during the early 1980s. Only recently have studies appeared that analyze data from the mid- and late 1980s. (Edmonston and Passel, 1994, contains a collection of empirical analyses based on more recent data.) The question that remains unanswered is whether similar effects would be observed during periods of greater immigration and slower economic growth. Given that these are precisely the conditions that have emerged in recent years, the issue of the country's capacity to absorb immigration continues to be a significant policy question. In the past, the implications of immigration have most frequently been addressed in terms of population growth and much less frequently in terms of economic growth (Borjas and Tienda, 1987).

The slowdown in the growth rate of the civilian labor force, in combination with the continuing increase in the growth rate of immigration, poses challenges for both analysts and policy makers (see Table 1). These challenges derive from circumstances that are currently even more severe than the above-mentioned rates of change for the decade of the 1980s. Since 1989, virtually no growth has occurred in the number of employed people in the United States. Over roughly the period 1989 to 1992, total legal immigration increased (over the previous three years) by about 140 percent, although non-IRCA-related immigration has increased by only about 7 percent. Whereas new research based on more recent and perhaps better data for local labor markets may continue to show that immigration exerts relatively negligible labor market effects, under conditions of slow economic growth the public may well conclude that employment growth has not created sufficient jobs for both natives and new immigrants. That may well be the case even if new evidence indicates that proportionately more jobs are being created with than without immigration.

These circumstances raise issues for the perceived legitimacy of the social contract. Specifically, what kinds of people are perceived as having access to what appears to be an increasingly scarce supply of jobs? This issue is particularly acute when illegal aliens are one source of labor seeking access to jobs. Many observers have argued that an integral part of the country's social contract concerning immigration consists of an implicit agreement that good-faith efforts

TABLE 1 Percentage Increase in Civilian Labor Force and in Number of
Immigrants by Decade, 1950-1990

Decade	Civilian Labor Force	Number of Immigrants
1950-1960	12	14
1960-1970	19	32
1970-1980	27	35
1980-1990	17	63

Source: Bean (1992: Table 1).

to control illegal aliens are the price paid for the continuation and growth of a
moderately expansionist legal immigration policy (Bean and Fix, 1992; Schuck,
1990). The current social contract may have been rendered even more fragile by
the apparent failure of the 1986 legislation to curb at all, or to slow more than
briefly, the flow of illegal aliens to the United States (Bean et al., 1990;
Espenshade, 1992). Another exacerbating circumstance is that consistent evidence continues to mount that immigration exerts its harshest labor market effects on other immigrants (Borjas, 1990). In what is currently an exceedingly
difficult labor market, previously arrived immigrants themselves may come to
constitute yet another source of pressure to reform immigration policy.

Some workshop participants argued that the challenge that arises from what
are likely to be ever more insistent calls for policy reform is to chart a course that
avoids policies based primarily on narrow attitudes of either an anti-immigrant or
a pro-immigrant nature. Rather, the task is to develop an immigration policy that
gives recognition not only to the realities of a difficult domestic labor market, but
also to the fact that the immigration policies of developed countries increasingly
have environmental, developmental, and foreign policy implications. Stated dif-
ferently, participants raised questions about the need for U.S. immigration policies to develop in a context that also considers the country's trade, development,
and foreign policies.

The changing circumstances in which U.S. immigration policy is made—and
a broader context for the need for data—have two major implications for the
collection of immigration-related data. First, much of what is currently known
about labor market behavior and the effects of immigrants may turn out to be
period-dependent. Period effects may prove as important, or more important,
than other factors in explaining patterns of socioeconomic incorporation and
labor market effects of immigrants. Although the collection of longitudinal data
would be useful in providing a basis for estimating dynamic models of immigrant
behavior, hypotheses of period dependence need to be built into such models.
Second, data collection efforts in the United States need to be coordinated with
those in important immigrant-sending countries, especially Mexico. Almost all

current research on U.S.-Mexican migration, regardless of whether it uses U.S. or Mexican data, suffers from selectivity problems, because a portion of the relevant study population is residing in the other country at the time of the data collection. A coordinated data collection effort, with longitudinal follow-up of respondents, that occurs simultaneously in both countries would help to solve this problem.

Data Needs

Three recent trends in immigration influence the requirements for immigration data. First, during a period of large-scale international migration, the only measures of the number of illegal aliens are indirect. Although estimates of the foreign-born population can be of some help, they cannot facilitate specific estimates of illegal aliens, especially for annual in- and out- flows. Improved data are required in order to have adequate measures of this population.

Second, data about immigrants are incomplete at best. The decennial census showed more than 20 million foreign-born people in 1990 and could have missed about 1 to 2 million. The 1983, 1986, 1988, and 1989 Current Population Surveys collected data on country of birth for respondents and their parents, which are useful for tracking the growth in the number of foreign-born people; these data have been consistent with decennial census estimates. About 8.7 million foreign-born people in 1990 said that they entered the United States after 1979; this number is broadly consistent with other estimates, but there are some unknowns. For example, we do not know the proportion of Special Agricultural Workers who received legal status in 1986 and stayed in the United States until 1990. We also lack data sources on the potential impact of this program on immigration. We do not know about emigration from current data on the foreign-born population and their children.

Third, illegal immigration is likely to persist in the future. Martin and his associates (Martin and Taylor, 1991) have suggested that illegal flows will increase in the future because of the continued need for farmworkers and other low-wage workers in the United States.[2] Thus, the foreign-born population can be expected to increase, and its relative proportion in the U.S. population will also increase.

Current Population Survey data could be improved in three ways. First, it is critical to obtain information on nativity, including country of birth and date of immigration for respondents and their parents.[3] Such nativity questions would

---

[2]Although there are provisions for the "replenishment" of agricultural workers in the 1986 IRCA legislation, Martin and Taylor note that sizable illegal immigration of farmworkers continued after 1986.

[3]Subsequent to the workshop, several federal agencies cosponsored the introduction of a question on parental nativity on the Current Population Survey on a regular basis. A parental nativity question was included in the 1994 Current Population Survey interviews.

offer the requisite information for studying foreign-born people and their children—the two immigrant generations of the population, called the *foreign-stock*
population in demography. Second, increased sample sizes are required for
analysis of nationality groups and immigrants classified by labor force characteristics. Current Population Survey data can often be pooled to increase sample
sizes, but even larger sample sizes would be required to provide sufficient cases
for analyzing generational patterns for specific nationality groups. Because of
the high cost of expanding the Current Population Survey on a regular basis,
workshop participants suggested the possibility of an enhanced sample size for
the Current Population Survey on a periodic basis, perhaps once every three to
five years. Third, race and ethnicity information is needed on the Current Population Survey questionnaire and could be collected at minimal cost. The 1994
redesign of the Current Population Survey includes more detailed self-reported
ethnic identification. Analysis must rely on country-of-origin data to serve as a
proxy indicator for ethnic identity. No specific ethnic identity is available for
native-born people on the Current Population Survey.

AN ECONOMIC PERSPECTIVE[4]

Economic Trends

Since the imposition of restrictive entry quotas in the early 1920s, U.S.
immigration issues have generally been of little concern to economists. Immigration quotas and later the effects of depression and World War II produced relatively low levels of immigration, compared with the levels of the late nineteenth
and early twentieth centuries. During the 1950s, immigration again began to rise
toward quota ceilings, but fertility levels were high and immigration was a relatively low proportion of overall population growth.

From 1920 to 1970, immigration contributed a small proportion of new labor
force entrants. With lower numbers of immigrants, the foreign-born population
aged and period mortality more than offset net immigration, with the consequence that the foreign-born population declined during the 50-year period. Following World War II, fertility levels dramatically increased and net additions to
the U.S. population came principally from births, rather than from immigration.
Women became important contributors to labor force participation during this
period. What attention was directed at international migration issues during this
half-century came mainly from economic historians, who focused on the earlier
period of unrestricted flows, and from those interested in the brain drain—the
flow of high-level professionals from poor to rich countries.

---

[4]This section draws on the paper presented at the workshop by Michael J. Greenwood and John M.
McDowell.

Although relatively little work has been done on the impact of immigrants, illegal aliens, and temporary farmworkers in the United States until the last 15 years, there is now much more interest in immigration among economists; one important issue is the impact of less-skilled immigrants on the U.S. economy. This interest has been kindled by the highly visible debates on U.S. immigration policy, focused in large part on the legislation enacted in the 1986 Immigration Reform and Control Act and the Immigration Act of 1990. Renewed attention is perhaps also due to the fact that immigration is again an important source of population growth. Important questions also concern the possible impact of immigrant workers on domestic wage rates and the possible displacement of native-born workers from their jobs.

The focus of contemporary economic research literature has been toward the effects of unskilled immigration on the U.S. economy (Greenwood and McDowell, 1992). This orientation is due at least partly to a significant downward shift in the skill composition of legal immigrants entering the United States during the 1970s and to the presumably high and continued immigration of illegal aliens with few skills and little education.

Work on the economic contribution of immigration suggests that the aggregate impact of immigration on the U.S. economy is not large, for three reasons. First, immigration is large in absolute terms but small relative to the U.S. labor force. Excluding IRCA legalizations, recent U.S. immigration has consisted of annual flows of about 600,000 to 700,000. These relatively large numbers, however, are small (less than 0.3 percent) additions to the resident population compared with higher proportionate additions in the early 1900s. Second, immigration has offsetting effects. Immigrants may substitute for less-skilled workers, but they may also bring wealth and new, needed skills. Third, the effects of immigration become distributed and smoothed very quickly in the U.S. economy. Labor and capital are highly mobile and the effect of new immigrants, even if they shift labor demands in local areas, rapidly dissipate.

Immigration does evidence some negative effects, but the evidence is usually circumstantial. Some industries experience strong effects of immigration, with large-scale shifts in their labor force to recently arrived immigrants. For example, citrus pickers in Ventura County, California, and construction workers in Houston, Texas, appear to have been seriously harmed by labor market competition from illegal alien workers. Furthermore, offsets to negative consequences exist and often spread through the economy among other workers, employers, consumers, and regions.

Many of the available studies concluding that less-skilled immigrants have small but nonnegligible impacts on the least-skilled resident workers use data from 1970 and refer to immigration that occurred during the 1960s. Not only was immigration somewhat greater during the 1970s than during the 1960s, but it also shifted toward less-skilled migrants. The quantitative shift was due partly to increased admissions of refugees. The qualitative shift was due both to the admission of refugees and to changes in U.S. immigration law that occurred in the 1960s and became effective late in the decade. The changed magnitude and composition of U.S. immigration require analysis of more recent data. Researchers need to replicate much of the earlier work with the latest data, such as those from the 1990 census.

Data Needs

Several improvements in immigration data are needed for the study of the economic aspects of immigration. First, Immigration and Naturalization Service data are of major interest for economic analysis. Major improvements that would be valuable include the addition of collected data on schooling and language ability, assets at the time of arrival in the United States, and income at the time of visa adjustment.

Second-generation data are required in order to study an important group— the sons and daughters of immigrants. Understanding the nature of assimilation is important in order to understand the adjustment process for different nationality groups, and the second generation is a pivotal social group for studying adjustment. If immigrant quality (as evidenced by lower educational attainment and poorer job skills) has fallen, then there is a need to understand the generational differences. The 1990 census did not ask a generational question; it is absolutely essential to collect generational data on the 2000 census. The Current Population Survey has relatively small sample sizes for most special nationality groups, making even more critical the collection of data on the census. For example, only the Mexican-origin population in the Current Population Survey has observations sufficient for detailed study.[5] Third-generation data would also be useful, but their compilation would require collecting data on the country of origin of grandparents, which would complicate questionnaire design considerably.

There is considerable discussion among economists about the uses of panel data for immigration studies. It is not sufficient to collect data on a single cohort of immigrants. To collect useful panel data, different cohorts must be followed over time—but there is debate among economists on cohort interpretations. Chiswick (1977, 1978, 1982), in his work with cross-sectional data on white immigrants, finds that the economic status of immigrants improves with duration

---

[5]The March 1994 Current Population Survey had 4,200 Mexicans, sufficient for a detailed study at the national level and for selected states such as California and Texas. For other groups, there were 686 Filipinos, 650 Cubans, 338 Chinese, and 318 Asian Indians, by reported ethnicity. Some of these data are of sufficient size for national analysis, although it should be noted that the Current Population Survey is not designed to offer a nationally representative sample of smaller-sized ethnic groups, such as Chinese. The national sample might, for example, survey an ethnic group in only a few states.

of residence. Concluding in his research that unmeasured differences exist between cohorts, Borjas (1983, 1986) argues that economic conditions at the time of entry may distinguish immigrant cohorts and that the quality of immigrants (in terms of education and job skills) may therefore vary. If a longitudinal survey of immigrants were feasible, available economic studies demonstrate that it would be critical to design a survey that periodically selects new immigrants to follow over time, noting immigrant status at entry into the United States and all subsequent changes in status and citizenship.[6]   Such a survey would, of course, increase the cost and complexity over the survey of a single immigrant cohort.

Another important debate in the economic literature concerns the economic adjustment of immigrants (Borjas and Tienda, 1987). Numerous methodological problems have emerged in the course of this debate. First, census groups differ over time. Even though researchers have attempted to compare synthetic age cohorts, it is clear that differential emigration and misclassification confound the analysis. Second, native-born white men are often used as a reference group, further challenging comparisons for trends over time as the reference group itself changes. Third, immigrant cohorts change over time, through mobility and international migration, and these changes add complexity to interpretation. Fourth, research suggests that emigration has a generally negative selection effect (successful immigrants depart the United States more often than other immigrants). Some effects observed in cohort studies using census data may be affected by selection for emigration. To address these problems in the research, immigrants should be followed individually through time, and the selection process should be known. Such a longitudinal study could also reveal more about the remittances and transfer payments that immigrants make.

Finally, two other types of data would improve immigration statistics: (1) a question on precise year of entry into the United States on the decennial census and (2) data on immigrant status at time of entry and at time of survey in order to inform analysis about immigrant changes.

One of the most important variables for studying the economic aspects of immigration is occupation. The study of the experiences of immigrants must include the examination of an immigrant's occupation at entry into the United States, the occupational mobility that he or she experiences over a lifetime of interactions in the U.S. labor market, and the occupations into which his or her children enter. Better data are especially needed on occupational mobility, distribution, and competition. The Immigration and Naturalization Service should compile distributions of immigrants who enter for family reunification and employment reasons, not just data on family members. The analysis of the impact of immigration on U.S. labor markets requires documentation of the occupational

---

[6]See Chapter 7 for a discussion of the advantages and limitations of a longitudinal survey of immigrants. This discussion notes one requirement of economic analysis for such a survey.

concentration of immigrant groups upon arrival, changes in occupational concentration over time, and the occupational nature of competition for jobs among various immigrant and native groups.

The Immigration Act of 1990 tilts immigration selection toward employment characteristics. Although the United States has received more immigrants in the early 1990s than in previous years, they are a smaller proportion of the labor force and they vary by occupation. Immigrants are now concentrated in certain occupations, especially by countries of origin, and this occupational concentration can be extreme at the metropolitan level. Unfortunately, flow characteristics are noticeably absent from current data. For example, according to decennial census data, most Mexican immigrants work in only a few specific occupations, but annual immigration data collected by the Immigration and Naturalization Service lacks the detail on occupation needed to discern such occupational patterns for important flow information.

Aggregated, national estimates can be misleading indicators on which public opinion and understanding of metropolitan dynamics come to be based. The impact of immigration and illegal flows has varied greatly among metropolitan areas, generating public concerns that are not necessarily common nationwide.

For policy purposes, broad research questions should focus on several issues: defining occupational mobility for native-born people and immigrants in order to understand immigration effects; expanding the number of studies that focus on variations in employment conditions and the impact of immigration in metropolitan areas and regions of the country; conducting case studies in order to build up a stock of empirical effects; and sorting out the short-term and long-term effects of immigration. There may be short-term substitutability in employment but long-term adjustments in the labor market that differ in their effects. Research questions should also address the need to understand the relationship of immigration and economic cycles. There are potential fears of rising and falling employment perceived to be caused by immigration. Policy research must be very clear about the perceived and known cycles that the economy experiences.

3

Effects of Immigration and Assimilation

An important concern in immigration research involves the effects of immigration and assimilation on health, education, and social programs, particularly in areas of high immigration concentration. Much folk wisdom has viewed assimilation as a linear process of progressive improvement and adjustment to American society. The general assumption is guided by an implicit deficit model: to advance socially and economically in the United States, immigrants need to "become American" in order to overcome their deficits in the new language and culture. As they shed the old and acquire the new, they acquire skills for working positively and effectively—a process that may not be completed until the second or third generation after entry.

Today's immigration is overwhelmingly composed of newcomers from Asia and Latin America, areas with significantly different languages and cultures than those of previous European immigrants in the late 1800s and earlier decades of the 1900s. Concerns have been raised about the speed and degree to which these immigrants can assimilate—and hence about the social "costs" of these new immigrants—before they begin to produce net benefits to their new society. The traditional assumption is that immigrants have costs to U.S. society in the initial period after arrival, but that the costs decrease and the benefits to society increase as duration of residence increases. It is further assumed that the benefits to society also increase with greater assimilation to American culture. Recent research findings, however, especially in the areas of perinatal health, mental health, and education, raise significant questions about such assumptions. Indeed, some of the findings run precisely opposite to what might be expected from traditional notions and theories of assimilation.

This chapter captures the workshop discussions of the effects of immigration and assimilation on social policies and programs, health, and education.

SOCIAL POLICY AND WELFARE[1]

Immigration researchers disagree about many major issues that are essential for revising social policy, including the criteria used to admit immigrants and the extent of social supports required to ensure their successful integration. More specific areas of disagreement include: whether recent arrivals are less skilled than earlier arrivals; whether the pace of socioeconomic assimilation has slowed in recent years and, if so, why; whether the net social and economic impacts of immigration are positive or negative; which social groups and communities are the net beneficiaries (or losers) from the influx of new immigrants; whether legal immigrants, illegal aliens, and refugees face dissimilar prospects for integration in the United States and, if so, why; and whether the criteria currently used to admit immigrants are optimal for achieving social, political, humanitarian, and economic objectives. All analysts agree that reliable answers to all of these questions are necessary for future policy initiatives concerned with employment, schooling, and income maintenance.

Despite the many areas of disagreement among immigration experts, there is widespread consensus on three issues: (1) the volume of immigration is likely to increase over the next decade, (2) the demographic and socioeconomic diversity of the flows has increased in recent decades, and (3) currently available data are ill-suited to address adequately many policy-relevant questions about how immigration contributes to contemporary patterns of stratification.

Employment and Income Dynamics

One of the most serious deficiencies in the area of immigration and economic inequality is the absence of information about income and employment dynamics among various segments of the foreign-born population. Virtually all national estimates of immigrant employment, poverty, and welfare participation are based on data from the decennial census or the Current Population Survey. Although static measures of poverty status and welfare participation are useful for portraying aggregate trends and differentials in the prevalence of poverty in a given year, they do not illustrate the dynamics of income stratification processes. These tasks cannot be accomplished with currently existing data because administrative records on program participation seldom include nativity identifiers, and because nationally representative longitudinal or cross-sectional surveys seldom provide sufficient detail on type of program participation, much less duration of

---

[1]This section draws on the paper presented at the workshop by Marta Tienda.

episodes. Although the Survey of Income and Program Participation is suitable to address these questions and others about income and employment dynamics, items about immigrant status are now available only on the topical modules (i.e., questions on selected special attachments to the main questionnaire).

A review of the Survey of Income and Program Participation by a panel of the Committee on National Statistics (Citro and Kalton, 1993) recommended a number of changes for improving the survey. Because it is the preeminent source of survey data on the use of public services, information from the survey has great potential for contributing to current debates about the use of welfare, medical care, and other social services by immigrants. But to serve current policy analysis requirements, information is needed on potentially illegal statuses—a difficult challenge for any survey research. Workshop discussion did not address problems of such data collection, but such enhancement of the survey is worth further consideration. A further limitation of these data are the relatively small sample sizes of the Asian and Hispanic populations, which preclude detailed analyses of specific nationality groups.

Further advances toward understanding the process of socioeconomic integration of immigrants require a longitudinal analysis of employment and income dynamics. This is essential to determine if rising inequality among various groups of immigrants and their native-born counterparts results from greater numbers experiencing transitory or chronic episodes of joblessness, poverty, and welfare dependence. Studies of employment and income dynamics among immigrants should also help to clarify inconsistencies in current research regarding the relationship between length of U.S. residence and economic well-being. Longitudinal analyses of income and program participation among the foreign-born population are a necessary adjunct to policy because the program implications of transitory episodes of poverty and welfare participation differ appreciably from chronic dependence.

The Context of Immigration

Contextual analyses of immigrants' integration experiences are an important area of neeeded information. In practical terms, this means that future national surveys of immigrants should not only permit subgroup analysis, but should also represent the social and economic spectrum of communities in which immigrants reside. Whereas assessments of economic well-being based on national samples are worthwhile for broad generalizations about income inequality among nationality groups, they are inadequate for portraying the contexts within which economic integration processes unfold. Widely discrepant conclusions about the extent and nature of labor market competition between native-born and immigrant people illustrate the need to reconcile findings based on specific labor markets and those based on nationally representative analyses. In fact, the high concentration of immigrants residing in a handful of large cities raises questions about the usefulness of analyses based on national populations.

The context for immigration involves the entrance and exit of immigrants. It is relatively easy to see the excellent opportunity for contextual studies presented by a case in which migration takes place and immigrants settle within an ethnic community. Contextual studies are also important, however, when what is called the "quality" of immigrants is being studied. George Borjas compared recent immigration flows with those prior to 1965 and found a declining quality of immigrants in terms of assimilation and productivity. But the quality of an immigrant should be related to more than wages. Immigrants who came before 1965, many of whom were Europeans, came during a period of lower rates of immigration. Recent flows are different. Education levels of immigrants vary, and the averages need to be used in context for good analyses to be done. An illustration of the importance of context is the case of Haitian children enrolled in poorer schools in Miami's inner city. The education and assimilation experiences of these children might have been more positive if they had not settled in Miami. In summary, the context of immigration is important in research.

Comparing Political and Economic Immigration

Because systematic comparisons of political and economic migrants have not been undertaken, a third important area is improving understanding about whether and how the integration experiences of refugees and legal immigrants differ. Refugees undertake politically motivated migration, whereas immigrants have economic motivation, according to a perspective taken by some. Although the distinction between political and economic migrants has been greatly overstated, there is little disagreement that the reception experienced by these two classes of immigrants is dramatically different. Existing research is inconclusive about the effects of resettlement assistance; it is not clear if such assistance facilitates or retards economic assimilation. A useful experiment to resolve this key policy question would compare two similar cohorts of immigrants who arrived at the same time from the same country. The data needed to conduct even this simple exercise, which is fundamental for assessing the effects of resettlement assistance, are not available. Yet this exercise is particularly critical in the current climate of fiscal retrenchment. Between 1980 and 1991, the federal government appropriated over $5 billion to various forms of resettlement assistance, but during the past five years the appropriations for refugee programs have been slashed. The reasoning behind sharply curtailing appropriations for resettlement assistance for refugees, as opposed to extending some form of resettlement assistance to all economic migrants, rests on a thin research base.

Effects of Amnesty

In light of the increased attention during the 1970s and 1980s to legal status among the foreign born, it is imperative to investigate how immigrants granted amnesty under the provisions of the 1986 Immigration Reform and Control Act are faring relative to other legal immigrants and native citizens. Nearly 3 million illegal aliens were granted legal status between 1987 and 1988, of whom more than 85 percent were from Mexico. Despite great interest within the policy research community in the effectiveness of employer sanctions and tighter border controls, there have been no comparable research initiatives to investigate the experiences of legalized immigrants. How well is the legalized population faring in the labor market relative to other groups of immigrants? Did the change in legal status influence employment and welfare behavior? Although there has been much speculation about likely changes following the amnesty program, research initiatives have not matched the speculative curiosity.

Until recently, no data were available to investigate research questions about the behavior of new immigrants under the legalization program. However, the Legalized Population Survey, conducted in 1986 by Westat, Inc., under contract to the Immigration and Naturalization Service, provides a unique opportunity to analyze the income and employment dynamics of recently legalized immigrants. It is a nationally representative survey of immigrants granted amnesty under the 1986 Immigration Reform and Control Act. A second part of the survey was in the field in 1992 and should provide additional valuable data. This survey should provide essential information about changes in employment and program participation, including the use of several in-kind programs (such as food stamps) that might be traced directly to a change in legal status. Analysis of these data is a high priority for evaluation of the behavioral consequences of legalization on welfare participation.

Research Issues

Workshop discussions identified four areas in which better information is needed for the improvement of studies of federal programs and immigrant adjustment. First, improved data are needed about income and employment dynamics. The Current Population Survey could benefit from special-purpose modules that include retrospective questions on changes in economic status. For the Survey on Income and Program Participation, it would be helpful to have a question on immigrant status included in an early wave of the interviewing and to include contextual variables in the survey data.

Second, comparative studies are needed on poverty and economic change for immigrants in different areas and cities. Workshop discussion suggested that it would be useful to have a set of comparative studies on immigrant adjustment, conducted with common variables, for a variety of metropolitan areas.

Third, more studies are needed of the different types of immigrants in order to note the comparative effect of assistance on economic adjustment. Refugees (political immigrants) are eligible for different federal assistance programs than economic migrants, who enter the United States based on scrutiny of their ability to gain successful employment.

A final area that warrants attention is the effect of the legal status, especially legalization, on immigrant adjustment. A substantial proportion (probably one-fifth or more) of the current foreign-born population entered the United States illegally during recent decades, and many of these illegal aliens are seeking legal status under the general and special agricultural workers provisions of the Immigration Reform and Control Act. Comprehensive studies are needed of the adjustment of this newly legalized population, compared with immigrants who entered legally.

PERINATAL HEALTH[2]

Research is needed to improve our understanding of an important, contemporary public health enigma: the apparently better-than-average pregnancy outcomes among immigrant groups, regardless of socioeconomic status. Current health data on specific immigrant groups are limited (national-level vital statistics data lack information on immigration status), and immigrants' ethnic groups are often reported only for pan-ethnic categories (Asians and Hispanics). Still, pregnancy outcomes as measured either by birthweight or mortality are better among babies born to immigrant than to native-born mothers (Eberstein, 1991). Similar results have been reported for Spanish-surname mothers in California (Williams et al., 1986). Guendelman et al. (1990), using data from the Hispanic-HANES survey, found that low-birthweight rates were significantly higher for second-generation native-born women of Mexican descent compared with first-generation Mexico-born women, despite the fact that the latter population had a lower socioeconomic status, a higher percentage of mothers over 35 years of age, and less adequate prenatal care. The risk of low birthweight was about four times higher for second-generation compared with first-generation primiparous women, and two times higher for second-generation compared with first-generation multiparous women. Earlier, Yu (1982) reported that Chinese-American women have lower fetal, neonatal, and postneonatal mortality rates than women of European origin and those in other major ethnic and racial groups in the United States. Yu also reported that the superior health profile of Chinese-origin infants was observed at every level of maternal education and for all maternal ages.

Research in California over the past decade has found that infant mortality

---

[2]This section and the next two draw on the paper presented at the workshop by Rubén G. Rumbaut.

rates for recently resettled Southeast Asian refugees (especially Vietnamese and Cambodians) were significantly lower than those for the non-Hispanic white population (Rumbaut and Weeks, 1989; Weeks and Rumbaut, 1991). The results are noteworthy because the Southeast Asians had the highest rates of poverty and fertility in the state, had experienced very high infant death rates prior to their arrival in the Unites States, lacked English proficiency, and had the latest onset of prenatal care of all ethnic groups. Other Asian groups (Japanese, Chinese, and Filipinos) and Hispanics (mostly of Mexican origin) also had lower infant death rates than whites, and much lower rates than those observed for Native Americans and blacks. The groups with below-average infant mortality rates consist largely of immigrants.

The evidence indicates that positive perinatal health outcomes among immigrant groups are a real phenomenon, worthy of further investigation. Are immigrant women superior health achievers, even when socioeconomic status is controlled and, if so, why? What are the effects on pregnancy outcomes of a wide variety of sociocultural and biomedical risk factors for foreign-born and native-born women of diverse ethnic and racial groups? Although there are significant differences by nativity and ethnicity in pregnant women's histories of smoking, alcohol, and drug abuse during pregnancy—behaviors that are deleterious to the infant's health at birth and that appear to be more prevalent among the native-born—such variables do not explain other independent effects of nativity and ethnicity on outcomes. There is considerable complexity to carrying out research in an area in which immigration, assimilation, and health interact. Existing vital statistics by themselves will not provide the research answers; alternative sources of data are needed and should include qualitative information as well as new studies based on comparative longitudinal designs (e.g., identifying immigrant and native-born women of different socioeconomic and ethnic groups early in their pregnancy and following them through the first year of the newborn's life). If we are to add significantly to the store of knowledge and to develop a larger set of intervention options, such research and data are essential.

MENTAL HEALTH

Intriguing questions have been raised by research on the mental health of ethnic minorities in the United States, including immigrants. In a review of mental health prevalence rates reported in research over the past two decades (Vega and Rumbaut, 1991), studies suggest that rapid acculturation does not necessarily lead to conventionally anticipated outcomes, i.e., that improved adjustment to American society and a decrease in the mental health problems are associated with immigration. Instead, mental health studies suggest that assimilation—in the various forms it can take—can itself be a traumatic process rather than a simple solution to the traumas of immigration.

For example, results from the Hispanic-HANES study (Moscicki et al., 1989), with an exceptionally large regional sample, indicate low symptom levels of mental health disorders for Mexican-Americans in the southwestern United States and significantly lower rates of depressive symptoms and major depression for Cubans in Miami, compared with all other Hispanic groups. The Los Angeles Epidemiological Catchment Areas study also reported lower rates of major depression among Mexican-Americans than among non-Hispanic whites (Karno et al., 1987). Significantly, among Mexican-Americans, immigrants had lower rates of lifetime major depression than native-born people of Mexican descent; and among Mexican immigrants, the higher the level of acculturation, the higher was the prevalence of various types of psychiatric disorder (Burnam et al., 1987). Furthermore, the native-born Mexican-Americans and non-Hispanic whites were much more likely than immigrants to be drug abusers.

Other suggestions for future research emerged from the workshop discussions. Research should take the social and historical contexts of immigrants fully into account, in terms of entries, exits, and assimilation. And among nonimmigrant ethnic and racial groups, studies need to distinguish between different American-born generations (how many generations have passed since the immigration?) and conceptualize categories of race and ethnicity as social processes, rather than fixed, purely ascriptive categories. Moreover, research is needed to identify protective factors that appear to reduce mental health problems within diverse ethnic minority groups; recent findings show that certain immigrant groups exhibit lower symptom levels of psychiatric disorders than do majority group natives. Longitudinal studies are especially needed to characterize and investigate stress and its temporal patterning among immigrant groups, including patterns of immigrant adaptation to specific conditions of life change and their psychological or emotional sequence. And, given the unprecedented racial and ethnic diversification of the U.S. population as a result of sharply increased immigration from Asia and Latin America, research is needed to investigate the mental health consequences of racial and ethnic discrimination, and how different groups (especially first and second immigrant generations) perceive and react to discrimination.

EDUCATIONAL ATTAINMENT

The rapid surge of recent immigration has been accompanied by a rapid growth in the research literature on the educational attainment of immigrants; the research has concentrated predominantly on the educational levels of adult immigrants of working ages. Relatively little study has been given to the educational achievements of the U.S.-born second generation—the sons and daughters of immigrants—despite the fact that immigrant children are a highly visible presence in the schools now and they will represent a sizable component of the next generation of U.S. residents. The patterns of their educational attainment, language shift, and psychological adaptation cannot be predicted on the basis of their parents' performance, nor from the experience of earlier waves of large-scale immigration. Research on the children of immigrants poses significant but so far unanswered theoretical and empirical questions. What factors account for variations in successful English-language acquisition for the children of immigrants? What is the role of family factors (encouragement of regular study and the setting of education and occupation goals, for example) for educational attainment?

Available results from the limited studies available are suggestive. In a study of students in the San Diego high schools, lower grade point averages were noted for Hispanics, Pacific Islanders, and blacks than for all other students. With the exception of Hispanics, immigrant minority students from non-English-speaking families had higher grade averages than either majority native-born students or immigrant minority students from English-speaking families. The highest grade point averages were those of students in immigrant families from China, Korea, Japan, Vietnam, and the Philippines. More remarkably, Hmong students (whose parents are largely illiterate peasants from the Laotian highlands) and Cambodian students (whose parents are mostly from poorly educated rural areas) were outperforming the average native-born student. Other research has reported similar findings among immigrants of lower socioeconomic status from Central America, Southeast Asia, and the Punjab, and similar studies have found that Mexican-born immigrant students do better in school and are less likely to drop out than U.S.-born students of Mexican descent, despite the comparatively greater socioeconomic disadvantages of less assimilated foreign-born people (Rumbaut, 1990).

Studying the adaptation process of immigrant children—patterns of language acquisition, educational attainment, cultural and psychological adjustment, ethnic identity, and acculturation strategies—can best be approached through comparative longitudinal research designs in a variety of community contexts, supplemented by intensive ethnographic field work. Parental socioeconomic status and individual human capital can certainly be expected to have a strong effect on every aspect of the adaptation process, but those characteristics and related demographic variables cannot by themselves provide a completely satisfactory explanation. For that purpose, existing data sets are not adequate to the research tasks. Data are needed on the different contexts of reception and incorporation facing different immigrant groups, including the presence or absence of discrimination and the character of the ethnic communities in which immigrant children are raised. Such data would be further enhanced if information on schools and the school environment were collected.

RESEARCH NEEDS

In studying the effects of immigrants on American society, as well as the effects of American society on immigrants, better information is needed in five areas:

• The predominant portion of immigration studies has focused on the problems arising from immigration. Studies are needed that examine the overall effects of immigration, not just the negative impacts.

• There is a difference between cultural assimilation (e.g., learning English and feeling at home in American society) and structural assimilation (e.g., achieving economic success). In addition, assimilation is a "segmented" process, depending on the subculture of American society in which different immigrant groups reside (e.g., ethnic enclaves, segregated inner cities, white middle-class suburbs). Several aspects of assimilation are essential to study: taking on aspects of the destination community, adaptation to new social and economic characteristics (compared with those of the country of origin), and integration into the destination community. Cultural assimilation does not necessarily lead to structural assimilation. There is a need to study the relationship of cultural and structural adjustment in more detailed studies of nationality groups than has been done to date.

• Available studies have examined changes by age groups of immigrants, but data have been missing on the temporal and local-area contexts of individual assimilation. Further studies (similar to Tienda, 1992) are needed on immigrants and labor markets, with data on contextual aspects, temporal shifts, and labor market differentials.

• Available studies suggest that immigrants have lower mortality and morbidity compared with the native-born U.S. population. Fuller explanation of mortality and morbidity adjustment requires improvement of data on multiple causes of death, duration of residence of immigrants in the United States, and the residential context. These data, however, may be expensive to collect if they begin as new data collection systems; more study is called for on the benefits of such studies, relative to their costs.[3]

• For studies of the well-being of immigrants and their children, it is critical to have data on two items. First, country of origin is important because some immigrants originate in conditions with high mortality: survivors of high mortality are quite selective and may be seen as healthier in their years after arrival in the United States. Second, the local context of their destination community can influence health outcomes. Information on conditions for both the originating and destination communities are needed for interpreting health data.

Workshop participants observed that there is a need for further research on immigrant adjustment and the policies necessary for improved adjustment by

---

[3]There are examples of ways to improve data sources without beginning new data collection systems. The Comprehensive Perinatal Programs in California and elsewhere have collected extensive, high-quality data. Identifying such programs may be useful in order to computerize the existing data for research uses inexpensively.

immigrants. Policy analysis requires improved information on, for example, the speed of adjustment to jobs, English language abilities, fertility changes, and individual endowments and community context.

Workshop discussion suggested that additional research is needed on immigrant assimilation and federal programs. First, workshop participants emphasized the need for contextual analysis, work that takes into account situations in which immigrants differ by type of entry and type of environment. Second, a moderate proportion of immigrants return to their countries of origin. Studies of return migration could provide useful insights into assimilation (or, in some cases, lack of assimilation). Third, different types of immigrants face different eligibility rules for welfare participation. Useful comparative studies of recent immigrants could be conducted that take advantage of the natural variation in welfare eligibility. Fourth, the visa category of immigrant entry is important for policy studies on the effects of immigration because the characteristics of legal immigration are affected by the number of visas issued. The decennial census and the Current Population Survey are not appropriate for collecting immigration status, however, because they are self-administered (respondents often do not know their specific immigrant status) and questions on immigration status on the Current Population Survey could affect the collection of employment data. Expanded data on immigration status could be collected better on special surveys or in conjunction with linked Immigration and Naturalization Service administration records. Fifth, most new immigrants in recent decades are members of racial and ethnic minorities. This introduces a new and complicated context for immigration studies, with the requirement for information on racial identity in conjunction with the analysis of other immigrant characteristics.

DATA NEEDS

In the absence of a longitudinal survey of immigrants that would permit the estimation of duration models, the decennial census and the Current Population Survey are the primary instruments for analyzing the impacts of immigration. Modest revisions to both instruments with data on place of birth, citizenship, and year of arrival would greatly enhance the range of possible analyses.

It would also be worthwhile to add questions on immigration status to the core questionnaire for the Survey of Income and Program Participation, rather than limiting these questions to the topical modules. However, simply distinguishing immigrants from natives will not further the understanding of integration processes unless additional questions about immigration histories (especially the first and most recent arrival) are included as well. The Survey of Income and Program Participation is uniquely suited to examine employment and income dynamics over short durations, but it would be less successful in portraying long-term experiences of successive cohorts of immigrants, even if sample sizes were sufficient for subgroup analyses. Furthermore, contextually based analyses are virtually impossible with the Survey of Income and Program Participation.

To aid in monitoring the self-sufficiency of refugees, the Office of Refugee Resettlement in the U.S. Department of Health and Human Services has conducted a national survey of Southeast Asian refugees, which has proven invaluable for monitoring the economic progress of political immigrants. The Annual Survey of Refugees was converted to a longitudinal survey beginning with the 1984 interviews, tracking a randomly sampled group of refugees over their initial five years in the country. The survey permits comparisons of refugees arriving in different years and hence allows an evaluation of the relative influence of changing conditions of the period on the process of economic and social integration.

The survey would be strengthened if two changes were made. First, the length of time refugee families are followed should be extended from the current 5 to at least 10 years. This is necessary because, at least in California, a significant share of the refugee population had not exited welfare after five years of U.S. residence. Because many refugees remained dependent on welfare at the end of the study period, the data analysis is limited by the small number of refugees who have made the transition to work and adequate income. Second, it would be useful to include other entrants (such as Haitian and Cuban [Mariel] "entrants," even though they did not enter the United States as refugees) in the Annual Survey of Refugees so that their adjustment experiences can be compared more systematically with those of Southeast Asian refugees.

Federal programs to assist immigrants economically began in the early 1960s with efforts to aid refugees from Cuba. These programs have continued, with an emphasis on providing economic support to refugees. Given the national interest in programs to deal with the economic situation of immigrants, the lack of data on the incidence and prevalence of poverty among the foreign-born population is a serious deficiency.

It is important to note that the adjustment of immigrants differs for legal immigrants, illegal aliens, and refugees—each of whom has different social and economic characteristics and different eligibility for federal and state welfare programs. Refugees in California, for instance, seem to remain on welfare longer than other immigrants. In contrast, the welfare participation of aliens legalized under the provisions of the Immigration Reform and Control Act seems to be comparatively low.

4

Labor Force Issues

This chapter summarizes the workshop discussions on the labor force issues of wage trends and newly emerging industries.

ECONOMIC ASPECTS OF IMMIGRATION

Economists have two interests in immigration: the labor market impacts of immigration and the progress of immigrants in the U.S. economy. It should be stressed that labor markets are not static; they are always moving toward a new equilibrium. Because there are both short-run effects and second-order effects, depending on the speed of adjustment in the market, cross-sectional data can fail to detect changes. The study of labor market substitution and complementary changes requires longitudinal data, which may tell stories different from those of the cross-sectional data.

There are two important areas for research on immigrants and the labor force. First, more work is required on the bounds and nature of labor markets. Labor markets have changed considerably in recent decades, presenting a changing context for recent immigrants. Metropolitan labor markets are now a prominent feature for immigrants, yet we lack a clear idea of the edges of urban labor markets and how metropolitan labor markets work. Conceptual work is also needed on the role of employers in metropolitan labor markets, how they recruit workers from within and outside urban areas, and how they affect labor force participation.

Second, there are issues involving ethnic groups in the study of labor markets. Current research often uses pan-ethnic labels, such as *Asian* or *Hispanic*, without a sound rationale for including many different nationality groups within a common category. Also, studies frequently use the group *white non-Hispanic* as a reference for empirical comparisons. Important questions for research are: What groups should be used and what is the proper reference group for empirical research on immigrants? If labor markets are structurally divided, as is often argued, what ethnic or country-of-origin aggregation is meaningful for comparisons?

WAGE TRENDS[1]

Although discussions of the economic assimilation of immigrants encompass several alternative perspectives, most agree on the beginning fact: in cross-sectional data, immigrant earnings are typically lowest for the most recent arrivals and highest for those who came long ago, compared with native-born persons. The first explanation for this pattern is that it reflects labor market assimilation (this is the view associated with Chiswick, 1978). According to this view, earnings of the typical immigrant rise quickly after arrival and eventually equal or even overtake the wages of natives. A critical concept for this first perspective is the idea of location-specific capital. Immediately after immigration, immigrants suffer the disadvantage of knowing far less than natives about the cultural, institutional, and economic characteristics of the U.S. labor market. In addition, their skills may not be readily adaptable to the new market. Consequently, their initial wages will be below those of otherwise equally qualified native-born residents. As the immigrants become better acquainted with the U.S. labor market, their wages catch up with natives, usually within 10 to 15 years after arrival. Empirical research with cross-sectional data suggests that the wage gap between immigrants and natives is most pronounced for immigrants whose culture and language are most dissimilar to the United States. The wage gap between immigrants and natives is smaller for immigrants from Canada and the United Kingdom, for example, for whom the initial differences are smaller.

A second perspective is that economic assimilation is largely a mirage. Instead, it is argued, the declining cohort quality of immigrants is the primary reason for the observed cross-sectional decline in wages for the more recent arrivals (this view is associated with Borjas, 1990). In this view, the reason that more recent immigrants do poorly is not because they have not yet assimilated into the U.S. labor market. Rather, their wages are low because more recent waves of immigrants are of lower "labor market quality" (i.e., have lower education qualifications and poorer job skills) than earlier immigrant cohorts. If the quality hypothesis predominates, the future outlook for recently arrived immi-

---

[1]This section draws on the paper presented at the workshop by James P. Smith.

grants is dim. The wage deficiency that they now face will continue with them throughout their U.S. labor market careers. This contrasts with the assimilation hypothesis, which promises a far more optimistic future for recent immigrants as their wages rise as they adjust to the U.S. labor market.

An examination of empirical evidence on the wage trends of male Hispanic workers from 1940 to 1987 reveals that they earned about two-thirds of the earnings of all white men during the period. There was also an increase since 1970 in the proportion of Hispanic men living in poverty, following a long-term decline since 1940. At present, there is a higher proportion of Hispanic men living in poverty than black men. In 1940 black men earned about two-thirds of what Hispanic men earned in 1940; they now earn more. The first explanation for this pattern is that it indeed reflects labor market assimilation, with the earnings of the typical Hispanic male immigrant rising quickly after his arrival and eventually equaling the wages of natives. The alternative view is that their wages are low because more recent immigrant cohorts are of lower labor market quality than earlier ones.

Wage analysis focused on the life cycle of Hispanic men who entered the United States between 1956 and 1960, classified by years of labor force experience, shows an overall pattern of little improvement with experience. Educational attainment improves over time, but not as fast as it does for white men. The result is that the schooling gap relative to white men has widened. Data on English proficiency for Hispanic men demonstrates that there is a strong relationship between wages and English language skills.

Part of the explanation for the wage trends of Hispanic men may be employment discrimination. Hispanic men differ from other men in the labor force on a number of factors, including age, labor force experience, education levels, English language abilities, and place of residence. In work cited by Smith (1992), statistically adjusting for other factors explaining wage data suggests that a modest proportion (about 8 percent) of the variation in wage data may be possibly explained by discrimination. Apparently, discrimination is moderate, at best, for Hispanic men and accounts for little in the overall differences of wages between Hispanic men and others.

Percentile changes in wages for Hispanic men from 1971 to 1987, an additional useful analysis, lead to two conclusions. First, structural changes made it difficult to achieve wage increases during the period. Second, Hispanic immigrants experienced wage decreases during the period. Wage trends for immigrants can be affected by immigrants who have left the United States; in the analysis of male Hispanic workers, educational attainment was rising for the immigrant cohorts, so perhaps the poorly educated left. But if, for example, 30 percent exit, one would need to assume absurd changes (e.g., that only the poorly educated with very high wages departed) in order to produce the observed results (i.e., decreased wages, increased education) for selection alone—so emigration cannot explain the wage trends.

The main implication of this research is that excessive reliance on a single data set can be problematic for the study of wage trends. Because of the selection involved in immigration and emigration, it is important to study wage trends with data on individuals over time. Individual longitudinal data on immigrants would help by providing information on individual factors associated with wage rates, thereby enabling the direct study of selection. Improvements in the data collected would yield better interpretations, for example: (1) a census question about first and last entry to the United States; (2) maintenance of consistent data on Hispanic ethnic categories between censuses; (3) a census question about what work immigrants did before immigration; and (4) 4 or 5 retrospective census questions about prior work and occupational experience.

IMMIGRANTS AND EMERGING INDUSTRIES[2]

The response of the U.S. economy to the internationalization of investments and the growing competitiveness of world markets raises the question for research of whether there is a connection between domestic industrial restructuring and the employment of immigrants. Electronics, a critical sector in these global trends, has been characterized as an industry shaped by advanced technology and giving rise to professional and highly skilled jobs that require a well-trained labor force. A close examination of the electronics industry in New York and southern California reported at the workshop suggests that the majority of jobs in this area require low levels of skill.

This effort to document the restructuring of the electronics industry and its impact on demand for and employment of Hispanic women reveals a major finding: there is increasing change in the U.S. work force as a result of international competition. In particular, the electronics industry has been changing in three interrelated ways: (1) shifting to subcontracting and decentralized manufacturing, (2) expanding the informal stratum with the proliferation of small shops for industrial work, and (3) tapping a labor force that is increasingly female, with many women from minority and immigrant populations.

The electronics industry in southern California now employs a significant number of foreign-born Hispanics, especially women, in the lower echelons of electronics production. Of the direct production workers in the southern California electronics industry, 45 percent are Hispanic and one-third of them are foreign-born; more than 60 percent of the direct production workers are female (these percentages are higher than for other California manufacturing industries). The electronics industry in New York also relies heavily on ethnic minorities and immigrants, particularly from East Asia and Latin America.

The growing presence of Hispanic women in the lower and middle echelons

---

[2]This section draws on the paper presented at the workshop by M. Patricia Fernandez-Kelly.

of electronics production is partly due to changes in the composition of local labor markets in southern California and New York. The increasing number of Latin American and Asian immigrants makes it likely that many of them will seek employment in the various sectors of the economy, including industrial production. However, there is a high degree of selectivity of Hispanic women in the electronics industry.

Workshop discussion of this research suggested three implications. First, there is a need for further research into the process of immigrant selection within industries. The observed preference for particular labor pools—those formed by women, immigrants, and minorities—is an important factor in determining the locational choices of electronics companies. This is important because it suggests that not all workers benefit equally from the restructuring of domestic production and, similarly, not all will benefit equally from the future changes of U.S. industry. Moreover, there is considerable heterogeneity of immigrants, with divisions into various social classes.

Second, employment in smaller companies provides an alternative to the traditional forms of large industrial employers and warrants further attention. The restructuring of the domestic electronics industry has entailed subcontracting and the streamlining of production operations. Production has been translated into a proliferation of smaller, more flexible companies and an expansion of the informal stratum. The trend seems to be toward the growth of smaller companies, some of which illustrate the advantages of flexible, specialized niches, and others of which are sweatshops that depend on minimally paid workers. The relationship between these emerging new forms of production and immigration requires study.

Third, the North American Free Trade Agreement (NAFTA) is altering the employment context for immigration, which will need to be carefully considered. Some observers fear that the elimination of trade barriers among Canada, Mexico, and the United States will accentuate the trend toward Mexico-bound relocation of the manufacturing industry from Canada and the United States. The electronics industry reflects the growing polarization of the labor market in the United States, with the creation of some professional and highly skilled jobs at the top end and large numbers of unskilled jobs at the bottom end. Along with garment workers, electronics workers are paid the lowest wages of industrial workers in the United States. The availability of labor pools formed by immigrants from Asia and Latin America represents one factor affecting the decisions of companies to maintain or relocate their operations. Domestic operations, with a proximity to facilities where new technology is being developed and to the domestic market, may continue as a complement to operations abroad, rather than as a mutually exclusive choice. Workshop participants raised questions about the possible loss of specialized low-wage industrial jobs caused by NAFTA and the role of immigration in the creation of labor supply for low-wage employment.

RESEARCH ISSUES

Workshop discussion on the study of the labor force addressed the broad issues of the study of assimilation and the labor force impacts of immigrant entrants. For future research, the topic of labor assimilation involves the problems of defining the concept of quality and of interpreting aggregated and disaggregated data.

Discussion suggested three topical areas for further attention in immigration research on labor markets. First, period effects are important, albeit sometimes ignored, for work on the impact of immigrants on the labor force. Prior waves of immigration often paralleled economic cycles in the United States and Europe, with people moving in response to prospects for better employment. Recent immigration flows have not paralleled U.S. economic conditions; in recent years, the United States experienced high immigration (compared with the percentage of the labor force in prior years, although a substantial portion of immigration in the 1980s was a result of the legalization of previously illegal immigrants) during a period of weak job creation. Research is needed on employment experience for immigrants, for common periods of arrival, during different parts of the economic cycle.

Second, there has been a lack of study of the niche impacts of immigration. The industrial and regional complexity of the U.S. economy is great, so immigrants may have had a pronounced impact in specific local contexts. Immigrants differ in their labor force qualifications and, depending on the local area, may differ in their impact on the economy. Workshop participants raised questions about the impact of immigration in local areas, where there may be large or small numbers of immigrants. Some researchers suggested that comparative local studies would improve the understanding of specific labor market impacts of immigration.

Third, immigrants differ in a number of ways that are important for labor force studies, including their place of origin, skills upon arrival, and their immigrant status (illegal or legal, and visa status for legal aliens) upon arrival. In addition, there are important variations in education levels and English language abilities among immigrants. Asian and Eastern European immigrants are more likely to have higher levels of education. There has been a continuing flow of professionals with advanced degrees in recent decades from many developing countries to the United States. Although such selection by education complicates the analysis of occupational mobility of immigrants (among other topics), it must be taken into account. Too few empirical studies consider the diversity of immigrant types, categorized in several different ways, or consider different types of immigrants in the labor force.

Labor force studies of immigrants could be conducted using several types of major data sets: (a) field studies using multisite areas, (b) special studies, (c) administrative record systems, (d) national surveys, using the Current Population Survey as the key survey (with the idea of perhaps incorporating an additional sample of immigrants into these data), and (e) longitudinal surveys.

5

Social and Family Networks

This chapter summarizes the workshop discussions on the importance of social and family networks for immigrants and their success in this country.

IMMIGRATION NETWORKS[1]

The statistics collected by the government on immigration are limited for many types of social science research. In particular, when migration is viewed as a process, the information contained in administrative records does not include the relevant data. Empirical work suggests that transnational migration unfolds with certain regularities over time. Following the initiation of emigration from a community to another country, migration has a well-defined tendency to become more prevalent and to broaden its social and economic base in the sending community. At the same time, migration tends to focus more selectively on a narrow range of jobs and destinations in the receiving country.

Such regularities have been evidenced by migration from Mexico to the United States over the past two decades. The migratory trends follow from the fact that migration affects individual motivations and social structures in both the sending and receiving countries, in ways that stimulate further migration. Transnational migration is a self-reinforcing process that develops internal momentum. As a result, migration becomes increasingly independent of the condi-

---

[1]This section draws on the paper presented at the workshop by Douglas Massey and Luin Goldring.

tions that originally caused it, leading to common empirical features across diverse communities.

Transnational migration may originate for a variety of reasons. Potential immigrants may observe wage differentials or employment prospects that differ between origin and destination areas. Households may seek to diversify risks to their economic well-being by sending some family members to work in different regional or foreign labor markets. Immigrants may be recruited by foreign employers seeking to import workers for specific tasks, or they may be impelled to move because structural transformations in the local economy eliminate traditional sources of employment. Migration may also be promoted by a variety of noneconomic factors, including threats to physical well-being by ethnic and religious persecution, civil violence, and local or regional environmental conditions (such as famine or drought).

No matter how transnational migration begins, the first immigrants from a community are likely to experience it as a costly and risky enterprise, both in monetary and psychological terms. They have little knowledge of the conditions in the host country and are largely ignorant of its culture, language, and employment practices. In most cases, they incur the expenses of the trip and absorb the opportunity costs of foregone income while moving and looking for work. Lacking knowledge about prevailing wage rates, work habits, legal conventions, and social expectations, these first immigrants are vulnerable to exploitation and mistreatment, particularly if they are illegal aliens.

There is a growing amount of empirical research literature on the migration process, reporting on Mexican emigration (Massey et al., 1987). Most emigration begins with people in the lower-middle and middle ranges of the socioeconomic scale, generally married men, who emigrate after recruitment. Such people have enough resources to absorb the costs and risks of the trip but are not so affluent that the idea of moving to another country to work is unattractive. The first immigrants are usually in their prime years of labor force participation. Men are better able than women to absorb the physical risks of emigration, and married men have a family support network that can offer some foundation for them while they search for employment away from home.

The earliest emigrants leave their families and friends and strike out for solitary work in a foreign land. Most of the first solitary workers are target earners, who seek to earn as much money as quickly as possible in order to recoup their initial investment, attain a predetermined income goal, and return home. They have little interest in permanent settlement abroad. Once more people have come and gone in this fashion, the situation in the sending community begins to change. Each migratory act generates a set of irreversible changes in individual motivations, social structures, cultural values, and knowledge of the destination community that alters the context within which future migration decisions are made. These changes accumulate to create conditions that make additional migration more likely.

At the individual level, participation in a high-wage economy encourages changes in tastes and motivations that turn people away from target earnings toward longer-term migration. The firsthand experience gained from migration makes the satisfaction of new wants increasingly feasible. Someone who has migrated and returned home has direct knowledge of employment opportunities, labor market conditions, and ways of life in the destination country and can use these understandings to migrate again with fewer risks and costs than before. Once experienced, migration becomes familiar and a reliable resource that can be used again as new needs arise and motivations change. From empirical studies in Mexico, it is clear that the more often a man migrates, the more he is likely to continue migrating (Massey, 1985; Massey et al., 1987).

During the first trips, immigrants tend to live under spartan conditions, sharing apartments with other men and sleeping in shifts to save money. They work long hours, have little social life, and repatriate most of their earnings. Immigrants see themselves as members of their home communities and not as participants in the destination community.

As immigrants spend more time abroad and as the number of their trips to the destination country increases, the pressure to bring along family members grows. The first relatives to accompany an immigrant are typically unmarried sons of working age, because they have the greatest earning potential and migration is consistent with their sex roles. Over time, unmarried working-age daughters are likely to join as well, and finally wives and younger children. As a result, the demographic base of migration steadily widens and the mean age of migration drops.

Not only does the act of migration induce changes in individual immigrants and their family, but it also changes social structure in ways that spread migration within the originating community. Each immigrant is linked to a group of nonimmigrants through a set of social ties based on friendship and kinship. Nonimmigrants draw on these social ties to gain access to employment and assistance abroad, substantially reducing the costs and risks of movement experienced by the earlier immigrants. Thus, the demographic base broadens, as many in the community begin to emigrate. A network develops as the community of immigrants develops ties at both the origin and the destination, the network offering a form of social capital.

Each new immigrant reduces the costs and risks of migration for a set of friends and relatives and, with these lowered costs and risks, some of them are induced to emigrate, which further expands the set of people with ties abroad, which in turn reduces costs and risks for a new set of people, causing them to emigrate. Once the number of network connections reaches a critical threshold, migration becomes a self-perpetuating phenomenon because each act of movement creates the social structure necessary to sustain additional migration.

If the process of migration continues long enough, eventually networks reach a point of saturation. Larger and larger shares of the transnational community reside in the foreign branch communities, and virtually all of the people in the home community are connected to someone living abroad or to someone with substantial immigrant experience. When networks reach this point of development, the costs of immigration stop falling with each new immigrant and the process of immigration loses its dynamism. The rate of entry into the immigrant labor force begins to decelerate, perhaps trailing off, at this point.

In a sample of Mexican communities studied by Massey and his colleagues, the prevalence of ever having been in the United States for the population in each community suggests that emigration began with men in the early 1900s, and some women began to go to the United States after about 1920. The pattern of emigration can be described in groups of low, middle, high, and mass movement (mass movement is defined as U.S. experience by 30 percent or more of the residents of a Mexican community).

The proportion of Mexicans with U.S. experience or with relatives with such experience increases dramatically with the transition from low to mass emigration. The diversity of immigrants with regard to age, sex, and household membership also increases. Geographic diversity first increases, then decreases with the low to mass transition. Diversity in trip duration, legal status, strategy, and occupation increases with the transition. At mass levels of emigration, some emigrants have become foremen with better connections who can hire members of their social network. This narrows both geographic diversity and the targeting of the emigrants. In terms of social class, emigration starts in the middle of the socioeconomic scale and broadens. At mass levels of emigration, many more immigrants are from agricultural backgrounds.

Based on the study of Mexican communities, Massey and his colleagues report considerable evidence of common patterns of migration that are in line with the empirical observations of other investigators. These results suggest that common migration processes occur across a wide range of Mexican communities, yet their expression is shaped by structural factors operating at the aggregate level. The next step of research in this area is to study the structural factors and population processes that govern the spread of migration within communities, seeking to understand why some communities rapidly attain a state of mass emigration, whereas others develop more slowly and achieve only modest rates of emigration.

IMMIGRATION AND THE FAMILY[2]

Family reunification and formation are the cornerstone of U.S. immigration law. A large proportion of visas are issued on these grounds. For an immigrant,

---

[2]This section draws on the paper presented at the workshop by Guillermina Jasso and Mark R. Rosenzweig.

the strategy of immigration depends on family. The family also affects immigration after arrival. And the family affects the children of immigrants. In short, the family is key to the study of immigration.

It is useful to highlight some ways in which the family matters for migration. In order to gain permanent residence, an immigrant needs a sponsor, who is often a relative. Another way to gain permanent residence is to marry a U.S. citizen— which might suggest higher rates of marital dissolution among marriages entered into for immigration purposes. In cases of marriage and naturalization, naturalization becomes an important part of family dynamics. The children of immigrants are important: there is a consistent finding that immigrants invest more in schooling for their children than comparable native-born parents. And U.S. citizens living abroad sometimes marry local residents and thereby establish a chain of potential new immigrants.

Immigrant success, and hence the effects of immigration on the U.S. economy and society, depends on who the immigrants are and thus how they are selected. It is not easy to obtain legal permanent residence in the United States. Except for refugees, legalized aliens, and the new "lottery" immigrants (i.e., immigrants who gain a visa based on the random selection of applicants from selected countries), the vast majority of adult immigrants require a sponsor. Under current U.S. law, the prospective immigrant has entitlement to an immigrant visa through kinship or occupational ties to a U.S. citizen or resident, who in turn verifies the relationship and petitions for the immigration of the relative or employee. The familial route requires that the prospective immigrant either already has or acquires the "right" type of relative. Appropriate U.S.-citizen relatives include parents, adult offspring, siblings, and spouses.

One of the most important policy debates about the criteria of U.S. immigration law concerns the degree of importance that should be accorded family reunification principles, which confer admission advantages for blood relatives of U.S. residents or citizens, over criteria that emphasize an individual's potential economic contribution. The fact that the economic success of immigrants, as measured by their earnings, may be importantly related to the route by which they migrated, as indicated by whether or not they had a family sponsor, is at the heart of the policy debate about immigrant selection criteria. Existing data, however, provide limited information for analysis of this important policy question. Questions on large surveys, such as the Current Population Survey and the decennial census, on the type of visa of the legal immigrant at entry, indicating sponsorship, could help predict immigrant economic success and provide important information on the determination of admission criteria.

Emigration by immigrants—the return of foreign-born people to their country of origin—is a neglected phenomenon in immigration literature, due mostly to the lack of data (Warren and Kraly, 1985). Yet emigration is an important measure of assimilation, and it importantly affects the net impact of immigration. Analysis of data for the period 1960 to 1980 suggests that emigration is substantial—up to 1.2 million permanent resident aliens may have left the United States between 1960 and 1969, and up to 1.9 million between 1970 and 1979 (Jasso and Rosenzweig, 1990:124-138). Thus, more than 40 percent of immigrants may have left the United States in the 1960 to 1979 period. Moreover, emigration appears to be selective: immigrants from Canada and Europe appear to have the highest propensity for leaving the United States, and people from Asia the lowest, with Latin American and Caribbean immigrants in an intermediate position. As a consequence, data on gross immigration flows, which are used in most analyses of immigration, tend to overstate the relative growth in the contribution of immigrants, especially the proportions of European-origin immigrants. Net immigration figures display a much greater growth in the volume of Asian immigration than of European-origin immigration in recent years than do gross immigration data.

Census-based data on the foreign-born suggest that emigration, besides being selective with respect to country of origin, is also selective with respect to age, sex, and schooling (Jasso and Rosenzweig, 1990:138-144). Emigration is higher for men, for example, than for women. But without regular longitudinal data on immigrants and without information on the role of the family in both the United States and the country of origin, it is not yet possible to measure with much precision the magnitude of emigration or to predict who among immigrants will leave.

Marriage to a U.S. citizen is a potential route to immigration for someone without the requisite skills or blood relatives in the United States or for someone from a country from which the number of qualified visa applicants exceeds country ceilings. And, indeed, as U.S. immigration law has become more restrictive in terms of both family reunification and skill criteria, the importance of international marriage as a route to immigration has increased. Analysis of data for the early 1980s provides a clear conclusion (Jasso and Rosenzweig, 1990): international marriage provides a way to achieve emigration to the United States when it would otherwise be quite difficult. More refined analysis of the relationship of spouses of foreign-born U.S. citizens, the timing of the marriage, and of subsequent marital disruption requires data that are not currently available.

The decision to naturalize is also intimately related to family matters. One of the most important rights conferred by naturalization is the right to sponsor the immigration of immediate and close family members; hence, naturalization may be particularly attractive to individuals seeking to bring in a spouse, parent, or other relative. The attractiveness of naturalization will thus depend on the visa status of the immigrant and on the number and type of relatives residing in the country of origin. The ideal way to study the naturalization of immigrants is, first, to obtain a family history that includes information on the location of the immigrant's parents and siblings and, second, to track the immigrants and those family members over time. Other pertinent evidence could be obtained by following a cohort of immigrants over time, using available administrative records (such a study was carried out for a 1971 cohort of immigrants; see Jasso and Rosenzweig, 1990:110-120).

In the long run, perhaps the greatest impact of immigration is the investments that immigrants make in their children. Workshop participants noted that, historically, the children of immigrants have been higher achievers than the children of native-born parents. Data from the 1960 and 1970 censuses show that native-born children of foreign-born parents have higher levels of schooling and achieve higher earnings than the native-born children of native-born parents. Unfortunately, the 1980 and 1990 censuses did not collect information on the nativity of parents, so these census data cannot be used to study this phenomenon for recent cohorts of the foreign-born.

A second long-run impact of immigration arises from the family reunification provisions of U.S. immigration law. Because immigrants are more likely to have immediate relatives residing abroad than are native-born U.S. citizens, immigrants play a large role in determining who is able to immigrate to the United States. It is thus important to measure the number of immigrants admitted by each immigrant (a phenomenon that is referred to as the *immigration multiplier* in the demographic literature). Whereas the potential multiplication of immigration visa entitlements can be substantial because of family reunification provisions, the actual number depends on the propensity of immigrants to naturalize and to sponsor new immigrants. There is currently inadequate information on the rates at which immigrants sponsor new immigrants and thus on the size of the immigration multiplier.

RESEARCH ISSUES

In discussing social and family networks, workshop participants reached agreement on five points, including topics not directly raised in the two papers summarized above:

• The environment faced by immigrants is important. Migration is a transnational process with lots of circulation. It is important to consider the beginning and ending of migration. Because emigrants are highly selective (usually highly educated in their countries of origin, for example), there are enormous problems with survey data on the general population of immigrants. Any cross-sectional data on immigrants must be initially regarded in the context of the recency of immigrant arrivals and their countries of origin. Immigrants are motivated by push and pull factors, especially at the local level. These factors affect the choice of destination, as well as the prospects for return migration.

• The environment of immigrants includes not only the social and economic conditions at the places of origin and destination, but also the family ties and the social networks of alternative places of destination. The social capital of immigrants constitutes the resources that they can bring to bear on economic success. Family ties can help the initial adjustment and may offer social capital for economic achievement.

• For immigration in the United States, the type of visa a person has and the duration of the visa status are very significant. Immigrants are by definition a population of movers, and movers are likely to be more mobile socially and economically. But the visa status at entrance to the United States affects eligibility for programs (for refugees, for example) and for employment (illegal aliens have a more curtailed labor market, for example).

• Family and social networks matter greatly, and there is a need to know how they work. Family-based immigration may provide additional support to immigrants; in fact, they may do better than occupationally related immigrants. An interesting idea for research is to make this type of comparison for a sample of immigrants.

Workshop participants noted some important conclusions about the study of social networks. Foreign-born families typically have a larger number of members, a higher proportion of relatives other than immediate family members, and a greater number of adults in the labor force. Whereas the higher labor force participation rates among foreign-born families help to increase overall household income, the complexity of family structure may limit the mobility of individual members. There has been relatively little recent systematic study of immigrant families. Foreign-born families experience both negative and positive outcomes, which would be revealed through careful study of the diverse ways in which they figure into social and economic adjustment. The study of the immigrant family and its consequences for assimilation is an important research question.

Studies of Mexican immigration to the United States illustrate that it is an evolutionary process that becomes self-sustaining. There has been an expansion of emigration from a broader base of Mexican communities. This pattern reinforces the need to collect data in the United States and Mexico in a coordinated fashion.

Some participants argued, however, that networks may no longer be so important a part of the Mexican immigration process as they have been in the past. The reasons for this possibility are as follows: as Mexican migration shifts from rural to urban origins, it is less likely that those leaving for the United States will be able to draw on community-based networks. Urban neighborhoods are not the kind of communities that rural villages and small towns are. Several new studies being conducted in rural Mexico suggest ongoing changes there, too: the village is becoming less the basis for family survival strategies and is more a place of residence, like towns and cities. The research issue is that not all immigrants, from Mexico or other countries, are able to use social networks. Rather, social networks are a "social capital" variable that needs to be explored in accounting for differences in immigration levels and patterns, as in immigrant adjustment.

Discussions with the Mexican government for more than a decade about cooperative data collection suggest strong Mexican support for cooperative work with the United States. A simultaneous Mexico-United States survey is a possibility now worth exploring.[3] More money for research is available in Mexico at this time, and there is considerable interest among government and university researchers. Mexico is an urban nation, and urban emigration from Mexico is an open issue for its future development. There is special value in looking at the Mexico-United States border because about 60 percent of the manufacturing jobs created in Mexico in the 1980s were on that U.S. border. In the context of emigration from other Mexican communities, the border area deserves further study for questions of the migratory movement of labor.

DATA NEEDS

The migration process itself provides an important theoretical framework for analyzing immigration into the United States. As described in this chapter, the migration process involves a social network, with the immigrant situated in a complex set of family and relational ties. The available immigration data from administrative records, however, provide information on individual events, abstracting the immigrant from the temporal and social networks. Whereas such agencies as the Immigration and Naturalization Service have a legal interest in such individual events as naturalization, federal immigration policy should also have a broad interest in the interconnection of events in the migration process, including what happens to immigrants after entering the United States.

If significant progress is to be made in the understanding of immigration in the context of U.S. immigration law, new data are needed that take into account the fundamental role of the family—both in the country of origin and in the United States—that follow the immigrant and relevant family members over time, and that are much more comprehensive than existing data in terms of immigrant behavior and immigrant legal status. Moreover, to avoid the biases associated with cross-sectional data, especially those due to emigration selectivity, such data must be longitudinal. Workshop participants suggested that one data base for studying migration processes would consist of an individual survey, drawn from successive cohorts of new immigrants (and possibly illegal aliens and legal nonimmigrants) who are reinterviewed periodically, along with associated family information. Currently, one principal data source for studying immigration is the administrative records of the Immigration and Naturalization Service These data bases, while quite valuable, have many well-known limitations

---

[3]Subsequent to the workshop, the U.S. Commission on Immigration initiated a binational Mexico-United States research group that will examine the advantages of a coordinated binational immigration survey, along with other topics.

that arise principally from the fact that they are not designed specifically for the study of immigrants or immigration.

Workshop participants considered possible improvements of Immigration and Naturalization Service administrative records for the study of social networks. There are some limits about what available records can provide: (a) not everyone wants to migrate to the United States, including people with relatives in the United States and people eligible to sponsor their relatives abroad; (b) the sponsor of an immigrant may be only the most convenient of many potential sponsors; and (c) occupationally related immigrants could, in some hypothetical circumstances, have entered as family-based immigrants.

In general, workshop participants urged the Immigration and Naturalization Service to consider enhancements to its the creation of family records. Linkage of current Immigration and Naturalization Service administrative records is feasible in general, although it is complicated by name changes in some records. Also, some records are not automated at present and require a search through paper records. It would be useful to ensure that key records for family study are automated for retrieval and possible linkage. The relatives of an immigrant present special problems because there may be duplicate records, with different relatives reporting on the same person. Increased linkage and exploitation of the usefulness of Immigration and Naturalization Service records would help to improve the quality of the records, including methods for dealing with possible duplication.

One item would be especially useful to improve and attach to the current administrative records: occupation both upon entrance to the United States and after arrival (at the time of naturalization, for example). Occupational data are collected at the time of application for a visa or change of visa status, and again at time of naturalization (for those immigrants who remain in the United States and seek naturalization). Occupational data are currently provided by only about 50 percent of the respondents. Little investigation has been conducted on the selectivity or quality of the reported INS occupational information (one exception is a study by North, 1995). Such added information, especially when more complete and linked to other records, would greatly enhance the value of Immigration and Naturalization Service administrative records for studies of the family and social networks.

In sum, there are significant enhancements to these existing data sources that could potentially produce large gains at relatively little cost:

• Creation of Immigration and Naturalization Service sponsorship files would provide machine-readable records for linking data on immigrants with data on other immigrants they have sponsored.
• Addition of information to the New Immigrant File of the Immigration and Naturalization Service (the principal's A-number, identifiers for both visa sponsor and financial sponsor, information on offsprings and siblings, schooling,

and number of marriages for self and spouse) would increase the usefulness of current administrative data on new permanent resident aliens. Although the collection of additional information at the time of visa application would increase respondent burden, it would enhance the research value of INS records for important policy analysis. Initiation of data collection, workshop participants argued, should include an assessment of data accuracy.

• Additional enhancements of Immigration and Naturalization Service data (inclusion of more occupational categories and publication of sex-specific counts) would further increase the usefulness of the data.

6

Immigration Data Needs

In preceding chapters, we reviewed the topics of immigration study that were covered at the workshop. In this chapter, we recapitulate the specific data needs previously discussed, with a focus on the recommendations for the improvement of current data. The data needs are grouped into several topics: the decennial census, the Current Population Survey, Immigration and Naturalization Service records, case studies, and data on nationality, race, and ethnicity. Chapter 7 discusses the pros and cons of developing a new longitudinal survey of immigrants.

DECENNIAL CENSUS

It is important to review the role of the census, the cornerstone of the nation's statistical information on the population, in providing immigration data. The 1990 decennial census included several questions that are important for immigration research: on nativity (place of birth of respondents), date of entry to the United States for the foreign-born population, citizenship, language used at home, English language abilities, ethnic ancestry, and race and ethnicity. Workshop participants strongly endorsed the retention of these basic data in future censuses.

A question on parental nativity (place of birth of respondents' parents) is an important one for the decennial census. Although such information was collected on the 1970 and earlier censuses, it was not included on either the 1980 or the 1990 census.[1] Parental nativity data provide the information required to examine

---

[1] The 1980 census dropped the question on parental nativity—the place of birth of parents—and added a question on ancestry. The 1990 census had a similar question. A question on parental nativity appeared in censuses from 1870 to 1970.

the social and economic characteristics of the sons and daughters of immigrants. Children of immigrants are a critical generation for study: they reflect the success and rapidity of adjustment to U.S. society.[2] The children of immigrants are a pivotal, young subgroup of a national population increasingly affected by large-scale immigration.

Workshop participants noted that further enhancements of decennial census data would help to make the census more useful for immigration analysis. The key needed enhancements include the addition of a question on duration of permanent resident status and a question on date of naturalization. Census questions require a strong political mandate for inclusion; for the 1990 census, there was no adequate mandate for including parental nativity on the questionnaire. The Immigration Act of 1990 now provides a federal mandate for additional nativity information.

Recommendation 1.   We urge that the Immigration and Naturalization Service work with other federal agencies and the Bureau of the Census, under the overall direction of the Office of Management and Budget, to include key immigration questions on future censuses, including a question on nativity and parental nativity, based on the requirements of the Immigration Act of 1990.

Participants noted the prime importance of decennial census data for the study of numerically small immigrant groups. National data on such population groups as refugees from Vietnam, Laos, Cambodia, Cuba, and El Salvador come only from the decennial census because there is no other cost-effective way to collect comparable national data for small and widely scattered population subgroups.

Discussion at the workshop included the topic of using optical scanning in taking the decennial census. The technology now exists for processing handwritten responses, and the Bureau of the Census is currently examining the possibility of using optical scanning for the 2000 census. Optical scanning would have several benefits: it would allow respondents to provide written responses instead of selecting precoded categories, and open-ended questions could be used more frequently. Participants were particularly interested in the usefulness for analysis of asking for the specific year of entry into the United States, rather than using precoded periods of time. Participants emphasized, however, that it is especially important to establish the scientific validity of open-ended census questions, if optical scanning makes it possible to have greater use of them. They also ac-

---

[2]Three book-length studies indicate the value of census data for this type of research; see Hutchinson (1958), Masnick and Bane (1980), and Cherlin (1988). Other studies include Hutchinson (1956), Massey (1981), and Portes and Bach (1985).

knowledged that census questions should be easily understood by respondents and that the form should be easy to process.

Mindful of these constraints, workshop participants strongly suggested that the Bureau of the Census should consider the optical scanning of handwritten responses for the decennial census. Participants pointed out that academic research groups have successfully processed handwritten records from the 1910 census. It would be disappointing if the 2000 census did not employ optical scanning technology.

An important source of decennial data for immigration research is the Public Use Microdata Sample (PUMS). The Bureau of the Census's 1990 PUMS files are 1 and 5 percent samples of the individual data from the decennial census. All individual identifications, including specific geographic residence, are deleted from the PUMS files in order to preserve individual privacy. The PUMS files are widely used by immigration researchers, particularly for the study of numerically small and widely scattered racial and ethnic groups. One valuable enhancement of the PUMS files would be to add such contextual data as local unemployment rates; the study of the impact of immigration on employment levels requires local-area data. Publicly available data from federal government agencies have limited geographic identification in order to protect respondent confidentiality. For example, data from the Current Population Survey reveal geographic identification of the respondent's residence for states and major metropolitan areas. Census PUMS files display geographic identification for counties or groups of counties (aggregating smaller populated counties). Researchers who wish to take the small-area context into account (such as the proportion of foreign-born people in medium-sized cities or rural counties) must have the macro data merged with the micro data prior to data release; they cannot create such data sets on their own. Workshop participants argued that such contextual data could be tabulated from the census and merged with individual PUMS data, at relatively low cost.

Recommendation 2. We recommend that the Bureau of the Census consider ways to add local-area contextual data to the Public Use Microdata Sample (PUMS) files. Contextual data on such variables as local employment, income, education, and racial and ethnic composition would measurably improve this important data set for academic and policy research on immigrants.

CURRENT POPULATION SURVEY

The Current Population Survey is the largest regular household survey conducted by the Bureau of the Census. In 1994, it covered interviews of about 60,000 households per month (about 140,000 to 150,000 individual observations), including the respondent and other household members. When a household is selected for the Current Population Survey and interviewed for the first time, the respondent and all household members are asked a common set of household questions. Selected information is recorded for each individual, including age, sex, race/ethnicity, and relationship to household head. The respondent is then interviewed monthly for the first four months, not interviewed for eight months, and then interviewed monthly for four more months. The interview schedule is designed primarily for the best statistical estimate of monthly unemployment changes—the main purpose of the Current Population Survey. The monthly interviews include special supplements, such as one with detailed income questions.

The Current Population Survey, which produces a great deal of valuable data, is the key federal survey available for immigration analysis. For more than a decade prior to 1991, the Current Population Survey occasionally included questions on parental nativity and other immigration-related issues. Parental nativity—and such related questions as citizenship and year of immigration—are essential for immigration research and should be included as key questions as a regular part of the Current Population Survey.

Subsequent to the September 1992 workshop, and partially in response to discussions at the workshop, a group of federal agencies worked to place a nativity question on the Current Population Survey. As of 1994, the Current Population Survey collects nativity information for household members and parents of members, allowing researchers to distinguish among foreign-born, native-born of foreign-born parents, and native-born of native-born parents. In addition, the survey includes data on the year of entry for immigrants and citizenship status. The survey makes available basic information on immigration for all survey months and for all members of the household. It is notable that these data are available as well for all supplements to the Current Population Survey.

Recommendation 3. The committees applaud the introduction of key questions on nativity as a regular part of the Current Population Survey. Questions on nativity, parental nativity, citizenship, and year of entry into the United States provide information essential to the understanding of immigration in this country. We urge the Bureau of the Census to retain these key immigration-related topics in the Current Population Survey.

In addition to the information currently available, workshop participants noted that priority should be given to the periodic inclusion in the Current Population Survey of other immigration-related questions, such as duration of job search, more detail on immigration experiences, and duration of welfare receipt.

Recommendation 4. We recommend that the Bureau of the Census, in consultation with federal agencies and immigration researchers, review the possibility of adding special immigration questions to the Current

Population Survey.   Additional, more detailed immigration-related questions would enhance the value of the Current Population Survey data for immigration policy research.   Such questions might be included in the Current Population Survey on a special basis, perhaps on one of the special monthly supplements, or on a periodic basis, depending on the purpose and usefulness of the data.

Immigration is too often measured as an event rather than as a process. Measurement of an event implies different questionnaire design than measurement of a process. From the process perspective, if a question on date of entry is interpreted to refer to the most recent entry, then the immigrant's experience in the United States would be underestimated.[3] If, however, the date of entry is interpreted to be the first entry, then their experience in the United States is overestimated. For studies of the immigration process, questions should be asked on both first and most recent dates of entry and the number of entries to the United States; such questions might be asked on a special basis in the Current Population Survey. Even better information could be gleaned from immigrant histories, although such data would be too lengthy and complicated for the Current Population Survey.

There was relatively limited discussion at the workshop about the advantages of enhancing the data on immigrant status on the Survey of Income and Program Participation (SIPP), the major federal household survey that collects information on individual and household participation in federal and state social services. It covers some topics of current interest for immigration policy, such as the use, amount, and duration of welfare. Workshop participants noted, without extended discussion, that the SIPP sample size is smaller than that of the Current Population Survey and would provide limited data for immigrants by country of origin, except for Mexicans. SIPP is a valuable data source, however, and the usefulness of SIPP for immigration research warrants further exploration.

Whereas the Current Population Survey is the key survey for use by immigration researchers, there have been discussions in recent decades about a joint survey in Mexico and the United States for immigration study.[4] Such surveys would have value for policy studies in both countries. They could explore potential immigration, immigration before departure and after arrival, and return mi-

---

[3]We understand that the Center for Survey Methods Research at the Bureau of the Census has conducted studies for the 1994 Current Population Survey of phrasing a question on the date of entry into the United States. Such research should provide better information on the respondent's interpretation of different phrasing and on more accurate methods for collecting data on the date of entry.

[4]We understand that a joint survey is being discussed by a group of Mexican and U.S. researchers as part of a binational study of immigration. The U.S. Commission on Immigration Reform is the designated agency for U.S. work on the study.

grants. Joint surveys have been discussed before in general terms; there may be a real opportunity for them at this time.

Recommendation 5.   We recommend that U.S. federal statistical agencies meet with counterpart institutions in Mexico to discuss the potential for establishing joint surveys on immigration.   Such a meeting should include key immigration researchers from both countries.

IMMIGRATION AND NATURALIZATION SERVICE RECORDS

Although some valuable changes have occurred in the Immigration and Naturalization Service statistical system in the past decade, changes since 1985—for the Immigration and Naturalization Service and other agencies collecting immigration data—also reveal that weaknesses in the data persist: the Current Population Survey questions on nativity have not been asked regularly, data on emigration and illegal aliens remain poor, and little is known about foreign students and new citizens. Some obvious opportunities for improving immigration data remain. Workshop discussion did not include evaluation of all INS administrative records (see Jasso and Rosenzweig, 1990), but focused on three broad areas for improvement in Immigration and Naturalization Service Records:

• Cooperative efforts are needed to improve immigration statistics. The matching of administrative records, especially records on program and welfare use, offers many possibilities for better immigration data. It would be useful, for example, to match welfare records to a sample of recent immigrants to make comparisons with the native-born. The results of such an effort would be beneficial for both the study of immigration and social program use.

• Coordination between the Immigration and Naturalization Service and the Social Security Administration could provide improved data and should be encouraged. Matching records from the Immigration and Naturalization Service and the Social Security Administration could provide longitudinal data on earnings for immigrants, an important but neglected topic of policy study. One possibility for exploration would be to assign a social security number to immigrants as part of the Immigration and Naturalization Service's administrative procedures. Such a step was recommended before—most recently by the Department of Health and Human Services in 1992—but to date has not been accepted by the Immigration and Naturalization Service and the Social Security Administration. A second possibility would be to take a sample of records on entering immigrants from past periods and link them to the Social Security Administration's records to provide data on earnings since arrival in the United States. With Immigration and Naturalization Service data linked to earnings information on individuals, dependents, and relatives, meaningful information on family processes would also be available for study.

• Conducting sample surveys of immigrants, using Immigration and Naturalization Service or other records, would add valuable information about newly arriving immigrants. There are special problems in surveying immigrants because they are widely dispersed in the U.S. population and are few in number in many areas. One possible survey design would be to use a sample of approved applications for a permanent resident visa—known as a green card. A relatively accurate address is provided by green card applicants. It would be possible to obtain information by enclosing a mail questionnaire, perhaps using several different languages, when the green card is delivered.

Workshop participants made suggestions for the Immigration and Naturalization Service to explore the collection of new data, including improving data on nonimmigrants, adding information on immigrant adjustment to information on previous nonimmigrant status, matching administrative records, conducting a longitudinal survey of immigrants, doing special surveys, and sponsoring case studies. Survey data on new immigrants, in particular, would offer useful additional data for immigration policy research.

Recommendation 6. We recommend that the Immigration and Naturalization Service establish the design and usefulness of a survey of green card applicants. A survey of new immigrants appears to be feasible, using the relatively accurate addresses that are provided by immigrants in order to receive their permanent resident visa.

A survey of new immigrants would provide cross-sectional data on legal new entrants into the United States. An ongoing survey, perhaps conducted annually or every few years, would also provide baseline data for longitudinal data collection. The workshop did not include discussion of specific proposals for such longitudinal data collection, although future study could weigh the merits and design for such a proposal. For example, should the survey of approved applicants be a cross-sectional survey to supplement administrative data on immigrants (e.g., collecting information on education, occupation in native country, support networks)? Should it be a longitudinal survey?

The workshop also included discussion of changes in Immigration and Naturalization Service administrative records that would lead to improvement. These records are collected primarily for processing applications for visas, visa adjustments, legalization programs, and naturalization. Although it is difficult to add questions for research purposes to administrative records, some simple changes would greatly enhance their value, including coding to permit: (1) easier linkage of the sponsor to the immigrants, (2) easier sampling of records, (3) easier linkage of information from the applicant and the sponsor, and (4) linkage of immigrant cohort records with other Immigration and Naturalization Service records for individuals.

Workshop participants stressed the importance of designing records so that samples can be taken from them. The technique of sampling has advantages because of the difficulty of adding information to administrative records. As a more cost-effective alternative, a sample of records could be selected for more intensive effort. From a research perspective, Immigration and Naturalization Service records are sometimes missing items for some variables. It is important to be able to sample from the records for follow-up surveys or linkage to other records to compensate for the missing information.

Working with Immigration and Naturalization Service records entails significant confidentiality requirements. Overall, the Immigration and Naturalization Service cannot release individual data for research outside the agency. Individual data on immigrants are not released, but the agency does release special administrative data, such as the names of newly naturalized citizens, as a matter of public record. For recent surveys of the population of illegal aliens who applied for legalization, it was necessary for the Immigration and Naturalization Service to obtain a special exemption for analysis by outside contractors. In addition, the Immigration and Naturalization Service cannot grant anonymity to illegal aliens who report their residency status on an Immigration and Naturalization Service survey. These special confidentiality conditions limit possible research activities by the agency itself and by others using its records; they need to be taken into account when future data collection is proposed. Nevertheless, it is important to exploit the inherent value of Immigration and Naturalization Service administrative records and to enhance them for better information for immigration policy.

CASE STUDIES

There is a long-standing debate about the usefulness of macro-level and micro-level studies in immigration research. Macro-level data—data for aggregates such as states or national averages—is useful for studying overall trends. But national averages are not always useful for policy research. Public programs and policies affect individuals more than they change averages. Some researchers therefore argue for the need for studies using micro-level data, information on such specific units as individuals, families, and companies. One problem with micro-level studies is that the subjects may be minor in the overall pattern. In the best-designed research, the results of macro-level and micro-level studies complement each other.

Within the domain of micro-level studies, there is special debate among social scientists about the value of case studies. In immigration research, case studies make specific inquiries about selected aspects of immigration. They are often directed to such topics as industries or areas in which problems are presumed to exist. A methodological challenge is how to interpret a case study: If the study area or industry was picked because of an existing problem, how representative are the results?

National studies often report findings different from those of case studies. In particular, case studies often find negative effects from immigration, in large part because they tend to select for negative effects. Moreover, it is easier to find negative immigration effects in local studies because positive effects often exist only for the most mobile immigrants, who are not concentrated in one place or industry. The more diffuse positive effects, workshop participants argued, are more difficult to detect in research data and hence may be a factor in the likelihood of case studies reporting negative immigration effects.

Case studies, with detailed descriptions of specific processes and changes, can be the point of departure for the study of new topics. Some researchers regard descriptive case studies as an early stage of work, and there is some value to this point of view. Case studies do not provide conclusions that apply beyond the subject matter described. Rather, they can provide ideas for further research to study and generalize. Nonetheless, good case studies can serve a broader role than merely the initial stage of research. A case study can have important scientific value in its own right, providing information valuable for specific purposes, even if the findings do not apply to all areas or industries. In arguing for a role for case studies, it should be emphasized that good scientific principles are essential to good case studies.

Currently available case studies, as mentioned above, have tended to deal with problems or negative aspects of immigration. Some of the physical and human capital benefits of immigration are often not mentioned in case studies. For example, U.S. residents get cheaper meals, better maintained lawns and gardens, less expensive child care, improved rural medical care, and larger numbers of skilled engineers and scientists because of immigrant labor. Some case studies focus on immigrant entrepreneurs. It would be helpful for public discussion if there were a better balance of positive and negative inquiries in case studies.

DATA ON NATIONALITY, RACE, AND ETHNICITY

Race, ethnicity, and national origin are major topics for immigration research. Studies of immigration by national origin (either country of birth or country of ancestral birth) often differ from studies of the "average" immigrant. It may make sense, for many studies, to focus on nationality groups, rather than to examine all immigrants combined. Adding Asian Indians and Chinese and Cubans together, even if they are in similar occupations or areas or social conditions, can cause problems for study and may not lead to sensible policy conclusions. Nationality groups have different origins, different experiences, and different conditions in the United States after entry. It is seldom reasonable to combine nationality groups for immigration policy research. Similar arguments can be made for race and ethnicity groups.

In this period of high net immigration, the U.S. population could include as many as 14 percent foreign-born in the first decades of the 21st century, due to a combination of low natural increase in the native-born population and heavy immigration (Edmonston and Passel, 1994). At the very time in which the United States requires more information on immigration and the foreign-born population, the 1980 and 1990 censuses did not collect detailed information on nativity and ancestry. Previous censuses asked about the country of birth of respondents and their parents, which provided information on immigrants, the sons and daughters of immigrants, and the native-born population to native-born parents. By contrast, the 1990 census asked only about the place of birth of respondents. This limits the 1990 information to examination of the foreign-born and native-born populations. We have discussed the need for more detailed parental nativity questions in the decennial census.

Race and ethnicity data are important for immigration studies. As immigration from Europe continues at low levels, the white (non-Hispanic) population is increasingly becoming a native-born population with native-born parents (Edmonston and Passel, 1994). The black population is experiencing its first substantial immigration in almost two centuries. The Asian population consists predominantly of recent immigrants, more than two-thirds of its members being first or second generation U.S. immigrants, and will continue to be immigrant-centered for the next several decades. The Hispanic population has more than half of its members in the first and second generations; this situation will continue at similar levels for the next 50 years, assuming current levels of immigration, fertility, and mortality.

The United States collects considerable general-purpose race and ethnicity data on its population. Basic information is collected on the Hispanic population in many large federal household surveys; limited information is collected on the Asian population. But there is little basic data collected on the foreign-born population by ethnicity. Indeed, the decennial census is the single important source of race and ethnic information for the foreign-born population. Mortality statistics on the foreign-born are believed to be poor. Fertility information on births to foreign-born women from vital statistics is limited; childbearing levels and patterns of foreign-born women can be studied, however, using "own-children" techniques with census data.

For basic information on the foreign-born population, the Current Population Survey is the best baseline data system. With the introduction in 1994 of questions on country of birth of parents of respondents and their parents, the Current Population Survey has the potential to provide essential data on immigration. Moreover, as discussed earlier, the Current Population Survey could also include special-purpose supplements in order to collect additional information about immigrants and their children.

Workshop discussion suggested two basic improvements to be made in current demographic data collection. One is the reintroduction of detailed parental nativity questions in the decennial census. The other is the maintenance of detailed nativity questions in the Current Population Survey, including expanded use of special supplements on topics of importance to immigration studies.

The significance of data on race and ethnicity is illustrated by studies of Caribbean immigrants, most of whom report that they are black in censuses and surveys. Studies of the black population in New York City reveals that the Caribbean-origin population accounts for one-third to one-half of the black population, depending on the local area of study. Many Caribbean parents have children now in New York City schools. It is important to be able to compare second-generation Caribbean black children to long-term native-born black children. The two groups of children have distinctive origins. Comparisons require data on the race and nativity of the respondent and their parents.

There are special challenges to the collection of self-reported race and ethnicity data for government statistics. One is that self-definition data depends heavily on people's understanding of the social conventions of racial definition in the United States. Immigration research provides evidence that immigrants may have self-perceptions and acquaintance with racial definitions that differ from those of the United States. Brazilian immigrants to the United States may wonder, for example, how to report themselves because the racial definitions in Brazil are not the same as those in the United States. Immigrants from the former Soviet Union have primarily an ethnic identity and often are members of ethnic minorities that are not specifically listed on U.S. government forms. For immigrants from the former Soviet Union and other European countries, it would more useful to collect specific ethnic identification.

Another challenge is that race and ethnicity are not factors in the selection of immigrants into the United States. The Immigration and Naturalization Service has no administrative reason for knowing the race or ethnicity of immigrants and, indeed, would be reluctant to give any impression that the race or ethnicity of applicants might be a factor in selection. Data on race and ethnicity of immigrants must rely on such other data sources, such as the Current Population Survey, the decennial census, and sample surveys.

7

Longitudinal Studies of Immigrants

The value of longitudinal data to the study of immigration is a theme that was sounded throughout the workshop. In examining the potential of a longitudinal survey, it is helpful to consider a taxonomy for longitudinal data (see Table 2). One type is *new prospective data*, defined as a new data collection study in which a selection of respondents is surveyed and then followed regularly over time. It has a heavy respondent burden, is expensive, takes a long time to collect, and requires a comparison group.

A second type is *new retrospective data*, defined as a data collection scheme in which a selection of respondents is interviewed and asked about changes in the past. A retrospective survey would select those residing now in the United States, would be cheaper, would provide data immediately, would have less respondent burden, and would show data on duration. A retrospective survey also has the value of providing baseline information, if respondent follow-up occurs.

A third type is *new prospective design with a retrospective baseline*, defined as a data collection study that combines a retrospective study at the beginning with prospective follow-up of respondents over time. This type of design is preferable to the first design because it collects past information on the respondents at the very beginning of the study.

A fourth type is a *prior prospective design with newly matched administrative records*. This design involves updating by linking the existing survey to recent administrative records.

A fifth type is the *study of synthetic cohorts in censuses and surveys*. Smith's

TABLE 2 Taxonomy for Longitudinal Data Collection

Approach	Description	Advantages	Limitations
Prospective	Follow cohort over time	Contemporary measurement	Respondent burden, expensive, requires long time, needs comparison group
Retrospective	Select sample and obtain data on prior periods	Cheaper, provides data immediately, less respondent burden, produces duration data	Data is historical, limited by respondent recall, some previous objective measures impossible to collect, potential unknown selection bias from immigrants who have already emigrated
Prospective with retrospective baseline	Collect initial retrospective data and follow cohorts over time	Provides past data for initial analysis	High respondent burden, expensive
Prior prospective linked with administrative records	Link existing, earlier survey with current administrative records	Cheaper, provides data for current analysis, low respondent burden	Current data are limited to content of records
Cohorts in censuses or surveys	Compare cohorts (not individuals) in successive censuses or surveys	Cheaper, low respondent burden, can provide analysis for long periods of time	Limited to cohort comparisons, possible selection bias

work (1992) illustrates this type of design, in which birth or immigration cohorts are followed in successive censuses or surveys.

ADVANTAGES AND DISADVANTAGES

Longitudinal surveys using a prospective sample are expensive and complex. Before undertaking such a survey, a clear idea is needed of its appropriateness for the particular questions being addressed and its advantages over alternative research approaches. Specifically, three important factors are relevant. First, a longitudinal survey needs to focus on a topic that involves change over time. Second, longitudinal surveys need a comparison group for the study. Third, a longitudinal survey works best when it measures an objective behavior.

The expense of a large longitudinal survey is another factor. For example, it costs about $2 million per year for the Department of Labor's longitudinal survey on labor force participation of 4,000 respondents. A longitudinal survey of immigrants would need to include the recruitment of a new sample of immigrants every two or three years, thereby increasing the costs beyond those of a longitudinal sample of a single cohort.

A longitudinal design with new prospective data is only one approach to studying change over time. As mentioned previously, alternatives to longitudinal survey data can be collected using retrospective surveys, such as in a life history format, or by successive cross-sectional surveys. Both alternatives are cheaper than prospective longitudinal surveys, although both have limitations (a retrospective survey would not include past immigrants who have already emigrated, for instance). Moreover, prospective longitudinal surveys have special problems with the reinterviewing of the original group of respondents. For example, the Panel Survey of Income Dynamics originally did not seek to interview people who had been lost in a previous wave; the survey now tries to continue the interviewing even if a respondent was lost in a previous wave. The National Longitudinal Survey of Youth also tries to continue to interview the respondents, even those lost during a previous wave. This seems to be a good practice for longitudinal surveys. Without it and with loss of respondents over time, those who are reinterviewed are not randomly chosen, and this bias is compounded in successive waves. The bias of respondents lost in follow-up in longitudinal studies can be minimized but cannot be totally eliminated. Retrospective studies and comparative cross-sectional studies have the advantage of selecting a sample that is representative of the desired population at the time of the survey.

An adequate comparison group is an important issue for prospective longitudinal surveys. What is the appropriate comparison group for a survey of immigrants? Depending on the purpose of the research, the appropriate comparison group might be long-term residents or citizens of the United States, the population of the country of origin, immigrants with different durations of residence in the United States from different countries of origin, or immigrants who entered the United States under different immigration categories. The design of a longitudinal survey needs to take the comparison group into account.

Successive recruitment of new cohorts of immigrants may be a better way to ensure that a longitudinal immigrant survey does not become dated. New immigrants could be added to an immigrant study population and then followed along with those already in the longitudinal survey.

With data on individuals, a longitudinal study would provide insights into emigration. Emigration of immigrants from the United States is an important concern (a substantial proportion, as much as one-third, of immigrants subsequently depart), yet emigration data are scarce. Following individuals in a longitudinal survey would provide data on the selection of emigration and factors related to emigration.

The contexts in which respondents live are important to consider in a longitudinal survey. Since immigrants experience new cultural milieus, it would be wise to ask them about their personal experiences and attitudes. Some retrospective questions, however, are difficult to ask on a survey—for example morally sanctioned behavior (bribery, embezzlement), deviant behavior, and the cultural aspects of behavior. Retrospective questions may also suffer from recall errors. It is important that surveys include questions on both behaviors and attitudes of immigrants in such sensitive areas as fertility and criminality.

It would be rash to attempt a longitudinal study of a prospective sample of immigrants without a clear view of the potential benefits. For short-term policy planning, there is little need for a longitudinal design. However, if the study focuses on change in attitudes over time or change in behaviors over time in both the United States and the country of origin, a longitudinal design is the most appropriate approach.

ALTERNATIVES TO A
LONGITUDINAL SURVEY OF IMMIGRANTS

Several alternatives to developing an entirely new longitudinal survey of immigrants exist. One could augment the samples of ongoing surveys. The foreign-born population is a special group, and one could oversample this group in an existing survey. For example, both the Panel Survey on Income Dynamics and the Health and Nutrition Examination Survey have added Hispanic samples to their data collection in recent years. Alternatively, one could alter the survey instrument in a current survey. For example, one could collect information on prior occupation, visa type, and migration history. One could also develop a new sample and a new instrument for the special study of immigration.

In thinking about alternatives, workshop participants noted six issues in designing a study of immigrants. First, panel data would be helpful in studying the adaptation of immigrants using a prospective design. The specific merits of panel data are described in the section below on special-purpose surveys.

Second, it is important to think about the sampling frame for studies of immigrants. Immigration and Naturalization Service administrative records might provide a sampling frame, but there are problems (such as the exclusion of illegal immigrants), and a comparison group would still be needed. Linking Immigration and Naturalization Service data is a possibility, but it might be legally troublesome. And, of course, the foreign-born population stock differs appreciably from recent flows; immigration flows shift year by year. Although recent flows have been predominantly from Latin America and Asia, such countries as Germany and Canada would offer useful comparisons for a survey of the foreign-born population.

Third, the social and economic status of immigrations is important and, in order to understand it, it may be necessary to oversample some groups in an immigrant survey. Some groups enter in relatively small numbers and may warrant oversampling in order to ensure sufficient sample size for analysis. For example, a survey may want to oversample entrepreneurial immigrants because they are few in number but enter under an important new visa category.

Fourth, data collection by the Immigration and Naturalization Service involves some special issues. It would be difficult for the government to ask survey questions that might have legal repercussions. Also, subjective questions are easier to ask in surveys sponsored by universities or businesses, since they do not necessarily require government approval of the questionnaire design. Certain information is often not released in government data in order to fulfill confidentiality requirements—another special issue. Data on contextual variables in government surveys are usually absent or minimal.

Fifth, data on duration of stay are important for some immigrant analyses. Surveys can obtain parallel lifelines (retrospective questions on migration history, fertility history, and so on). But it is a special challenge to understanding how to collect duration data on the migration process.

Sixth, ethnographic data are important to consider.[1] Studies using participant or direct observation can offer useful additional insights into immigrant adjustment. The major attraction of ethnographic field research is the comprehensiveness of the inquiry. By going directly to the social phenomenon under study and observing it as completely as possible, ethnographic observations can develop a fuller understanding of changes. This technique may be useful for topics that seem to defy quantification or in the use of self-reported survey questionnaires, for which nuances of attitude or behavior are critical and observation in the natural setting is paramount. Ethnographic studies may provide im-

---

[1]Ethnographic data are collected by personal observation by the researcher or research staff of people and families. Ethnographic studies differ from the case studies discussed earlier, which are of a specific research site (such as a factory or city) but might use survey data collection techniques.

portant insights, suggestive rather than definitive, although they do suffer from problems of validation, reliability, and generalizability.

Workshop participants suggested augmenting a large, ongoing longitudinal survey—the Panel Study on Income Dynamics—with a sample of the foreign-born population. A topical module could also be added to the first wave in order to collect pertinent retrospective information. This would enhance a current survey, albeit at moderate cost, and would initiate a longitudinal follow-up of immigrants with baseline data on such topics as past immigration, labor force, and family experience.

Other participants expressed reservations about adding immigrant sub-samples to currently ongoing longitudinal surveys. The problem, they noted, is that existing longitudinal surveys generally have not supplemented their samples with recent immigrants. Therefore, as time goes by, they remain representative of the population resident at the time the survey began. Depending on the level of immigration, they become less and less representative of the current population.

For example, although the Panel Survey of Income Dynamics is useful for analyzing black-white differences in income dynamics, its sample excludes immigrants since 1968. Adding a sample of current immigrants would not compensate for the exclusion of immigrants in prior years and would therefore permit comparisons only of current immigrants with those who arrived prior to 1968. A supplemental strategy would need to add immigrants since 1968 and replenish with new immigrants on a regular basis.

Similar arguments apply to the National Longitudinal Survey of Youth, which does not include Asians. Any new survey initiative should adequately represent the racial and ethnic diversity of the U.S. population. A key point of contention is whether existing longitudinal surveys, with potential cost savings derived from building on an existing survey, could be redesigned to offer an adequate comparison population for an immigrant subsample, or whether it would be more cost effective to begin an entirely new longitudinal survey.

Longitudinal data takes considerable time to accumulate for questions involving years of data. Another suggestion by workshop participants was to take a sample from records of earlier admitted permanent residents (INS or other administrative records might be used, or an earlier survey might provide a baseline data set) and interview the respondents in the present. This approach would miss undocumented immigrants, but it may be a second-best, less expensive approach that would provide useful information as soon as the data are collected and analyzed. It might also provide valuable information on groups of legal immigrants, for which there are important questions about adjustment in economic status, education, and social change.

Assuming for the moment the desirability of a longitudinal survey of immigrants, workshop participants discussed some important technical issues that need attention:

• *Sample size and coverage.* There is a trade-off between including more groups and collecting larger samples for major groups. Hispanics, the largest collective ethnic group in the foreign-born population, do not constitute a sufficiently large subsample in most major surveys. But a sufficiently large sample for specific ethnic groups would result in an extremely large overall sample size.

• *Visa status at the time of entry to the United States.* Status at entry is a desirable measure to collect, but it is extremely problematic. Using self-reported interviews, it is difficult to collect information on the various visa categories, participation in various legalization programs, and unauthorized entry. Much of this information can be found in the Immigration and Naturalization Service's administrative records. Even so, the use of administrative records would not include residents who entered illegally and had not participated in a legalization program.

• *Local labor markets.* Many studies on immigrant behavior, particularly those involving labor force participation, require information about the respondent's local labor market. For the analysis of such data, researchers need to have access to local-area geographic codes that would allow them to measure labor markets and other local context variables; alternatively, these contextual data need to be collected as part of the survey operation. Government agencies ordinarily suppress local geographic identification in the data they collect, which limits the analysis by eliminating contextual information. Knowledge about some local-area contexts is critical for questions about the economic adjustment of immigrants, but the confidentiality restrictions on this type of data prohibit their collection and dissemination by federal statistical agencies.

• *Sample survey design for reinterviews.* A neglected aspect of the design of longitudinal surveys is the sample scheme for periodic reinterviews. For a longitudinal sample, a more careful design is warranted than simply the notion of contacting the sample respondents every year or "every so often." The frequency of reinterview should be based on the assumption of stochastic processes of change over time and on how to sample from those processes. In general, a survey should sample more frequently for processes that are changing more rapidly. Thus, for example, for a study of immigrants, one may want to sample the newly arrived and/or younger immigrants more often because processes of labor and geographic mobility and education achievement are changing relatively more rapidly for them.

• *Respondents lost to follow-up.* Not all persons in the original sample can be followed successfully over time in longitudinal surveys. The loss in follow-up surveys presents both a financial cost (data are collected for which there is no subsequent information) and a statistical challenge (there may be a bias in those who are lost to follow-up). Although the Annual Survey of Refugees obtains respectable overall response rates and reasonable reinterview rates of those originally surveyed, there is some drop-off in the follow-up of individuals and families, apparently as they begin to move and lose contact with their original refugee community. A special concern in a longitudinal survey of immigrants is emigration: it is crucial for the follow-up to distinguish return migrants who can no longer be contacted because they have departed from the United States.

SPECIAL-PURPOSE IMMIGRANT SURVEYS

Although there have been few surveys of selective immigrant populations, special-purpose immigrant surveys can provide worthwhile information at a reasonable cost. For example, the East-West Population Institute has been supporting a special longitudinal survey of immigrants for several years. In 1985, the project began looking at Koreans and Filipinos. Korea and the Philippine Islands were among the largest single source of Asian immigration in the 1980s.[2] The researchers took an initial sample of visa applicants in 1985 in Korea and the Philippines. By 1988, 53 percent of the visa applicants resided in the United States and were contacted by mail. Telephone surveys were conducted in 1988-1989 and 1991-1992, and about 13 percent of the original visa applicants were still in the survey.

This longitudinal survey looked at employment and self-employment information, gathered as retrospective data at the first interview. This type of prospective study of immigrants poses several challenges: it is very time-consuming, with long periods before data are available to analyze. It requires a strong central staff in order to continue the data collection. Attrition from the original group of respondents can limit the usefulness of the data.

Special-purpose immigrant surveys are not as expensive as large national surveys and can allow experimentation with new survey techniques or limit attention to a specific population group or topic of study. They are especially valuable for studies with a local focus. Workshop participants encouraged the development of new special-purpose immigration surveys.

NEED FOR LONGITUDINAL DATA

Workshop participants considered whether a special longitudinal survey of immigrants should be pursued, recognizing that a new prospective survey would be expensive yet would yield valuable data. They also acknowledged that it would take many years before data on temporal changes are available, yet researchers and policy makers in the year 2000 would be grateful if data collection were to begin now.

---

[2]Immigration from Korea has declined considerably from the level of the mid-1980s. The Philippines remains one of the largest single-country sources of Asian immigration. In the 1990s, China, India, and Vietnam provided the largest sources of Asian immigrants—although the annual number of entrants fluctuates a great deal by country.

TABLE 3   Existing Longitudinal Surveys with an Immigrant Component

Survey	Description
Survey of Income and Program Participation (SIPP)	A continuing household survey on people's economic well-being and the receipt of assistance from government programs designed to measure short spells of need and program use. Supplemental questions on the 2nd interview include migration history
Panel Study of Income Dynamics (PSID)	A continuing intergenerational survey of families on demographic, economic, family structure, composition and sources of income, housing, and health issues information (sample of Latinos added in 1990)
National Longitudinal Survey of Youth (NLSY)	National random sample of youth on a wide range of variables, including labor market experience, marital status, education, and health. Oversamples Hispanic, black, and economically disadvantaged
National Education Longitudinal Study (NELS)	A continuing survey that provides trend data about critical transition experiences by young people as they develop, attend school, and embark on careers. The survey furnishes information on how school policies, teacher practices, and family involvement affect student educational outcomes
National Maternal and Infant Health Survey	Broad-spectrum survey aimed at augmenting birth certificate information. Collected data covered income, entitlement, social support, depression, prenatal care, hospital/health care providers, child health, child care, and use of federal programs.
National Survey of Families and Households	Survey of primary respondents 19 years or over, living in a household, with a self-administered portion for spouse or partner. The survey covered a broad range of family domains: composition, living arrangements, growing up, leaving home, education, employment, marriage/divorce, cohabitation, fertility, relations with elder parents, etc.
Health and Retirement Survey	Data collection focused on retirement decisions, recognizing roles played by: pension and social security retirement incentives, job demands and worker capacities, health and longevity, family responsibilities, husband/wife career choices, economic status, and housing and location choices
National Agricultural Workers Survey (NAWS)	Survey of farmworkers that provides data on the occupational activities of agricultural workers and families, job history matrices, descriptions of employment conditions (pay, health care, equipment, pesticide use), and information on social service use and work authorization.
National Survey of College Graduates (NSCG)	Survey of college graduates (identified on 1990 census) to gather information on education and employment history, merged with 1990 long form census data. Oversampled scientists and engineers.

Survey Dates	Original Panel Sample Size	Foreign-Born in Sample[a]
1983 to present; panel interviewed every 4 months for 32 months. Rotating panel design	21,000 households	1991 topical migration module: 10.6%
1968 to present	16,000 individuals	1990 sample added 7,500 Latinos to the original sample; many were native born
1979 to present	12,686 individuals who were ages 14-21 in the year 1979	874 in 1979; 644 in 1990, when immigration module was added
1988 (8th grade) 1990 (l0th grade) 1992 (12th grade)	1988: 29,000 persons 1990: 25,000 persons 1992: 21,000 persons	Foreign born: 6.6 % plus 0.3 % Puerto Ricans
1988 (at birth) follow-up in 1991; planning a 1997-98 survey follow-up	9,953 live births 5,332 fetal deaths 3,309 infant deaths	None. Children were born in the United States; some mothers were foreign-born
1987-1988, reinterviewing 1993	13,017 primary respondents (does not include spouses or partners)	910 foreign born plus 120 Puerto Ricans
Survey started 1992, scheduled for every other year for 12+ years	12,656 persons (7,600 households)	Approximately 10%
1988 to present, but longitudinal aspect ended 1992	Approximately 2,500 persons	Approximately 60%
1993 through 2001	151,000 individuals	Approximately 30,000

TABLE 3   Continued

Survey	Description
Survey of Doctorate Recipients	Ongoing survey of recipients of Ph.D. degrees in the fields of engineering, sciences, and humanities on topics of income and employment. In 1991, discontinued questions on foreign-born doctorates.
Comparative Longitudinal Asian Immigration (CLAIM) Project	Survey of Korean and Filipino adult (ages 18-69) visa holders (at time visa application made) asking for employment and self-employment information before immigration and in the United States.
Children of Immigrants: The Adaptation Process of the Second Generation	Study of 8th and 9th grade children of immigrants (offspring with at least one immigrant parent) in Miami, Fort Lauderdale, and San Diego, either born in the U.S. or having 5 years residence. The survey looks at models of assimilation among minorities, including language, ethnic self-identification, socioeconomic status, aspirations, social networks, and school performance
National Survey of Recent College Graduates	A survey of 1990, 1991, and 1992 bachelor's and master's graduates in science and engineering to collect information on long-term education and career progress of persons in science and engineering. The survey is based on the graduation lists of a sample of the U.S. institutions
Legalized Population Surveys (LPS1 and LPS2)	Survey of population legalized under Section 245A of the Immigration Reform and Control Act to provide Congress with a profile of aliens at the time of legalization and 5 years after legalization. Both surveys collect information on language proficiency, immigration and migration, employment, family composition, health insurance and child care, social services, education, income, and remittances. LPS1 also collects employment (prior to U.S. entry, at entry, and at time of legalization application), and health expenditures. LPS2 also collects employment (work history from January 1991 through the survey date, benefits (including health insurance), assets, and household expenses (to determine food stamp eligibility)
Annual Survey of Refugees	Survey of current employment or job search activity, past work history, income, English ability, household composition, social services received, and household use of welfare. The Refugee Act of 1980 requires that the annual report of the Refugee Resettlement Program contain an updated profile of employment and labor force statistics for refugees who entered the United States within a period of five years immediately preceding the year of the report.

*a*This column also lists Puerto Ricans in the sample, even though they are U.S. citizens.

Survey Dates	Original Panel Sample Size	Foreign-Born in Sample
Every two years, 1973 to present (two follow-ups each survey year)	60,000 persons	Approximately 20%
Survey started in 1986-1987, resurveyed in 1988-1989 and 1991-1992	Seoul: 1,834 individuals Manila: 2,077 individuals	All All
1992; Follow-up planned for 1995	5,267 individuals	3,194
Survey started 1992; every other year through 2001	28,000 persons	Approximately 10%
LPS1: winter/spring 1989; LPS2: spring/summer 1992. No further surveys planned	LPS1: 7,000 sampled; 6,193 interviewed. LPS2: 5,000 sampled; 4,012 interviewed	All
Survey started 1984; conducted annually in September-October. Rotating panel design with plans to continue indefinitely	Approximately 150 of each year's arrivals.	All

Several longitudinal data sets may already yield useful information on immigration. Following the workshop, National Research Council staff collected information on existing longitudinal surveys with an immigrant component. Table 3 displays information on 15 longitudinal surveys. Some of the surveys have general information (especially the Panel Study of Income Dynamics), and others have a special focus (such as the National Longitudinal Survey of Youth and the Health and Retirement Survey). Most of the surveys include a general sample of the foreign-born population, although a few are limited to a specific pan-ethnic group or to one or two nationality groups. Despite the fact that the sample sizes of the surveys are often adequate for general analysis of the foreign-born population, most existing surveys are not adequate for analysis of recent immigration by nationality group. Also, it should be emphasized that existing surveys do not include the special data required for immigration policy analysis.

The Panel Study of Income Dynamics (PSID) is one of the most valuable social science data sets. In 1990 it added a Hispanic supplement of more than 2,000 people (about two-thirds of whom were foreign-born) and continues to follow up these Hispanic families. This survey offers a pilot test of longitudinal data collection for the immigrant groups included in the Hispanic supplement. Only a small fraction of the Hispanic supplement were recent immigrants; most of the Hispanics in the 1990 supplement were survivors of past immigration or descendants of earlier immigrants. For a longitudinal survey of immigrants, it may be more useful to look selectively at very recent immigrants in order to provide data on current immigration policy.

In data collection for its 1990 Hispanic supplement, the PSID did not collect retrospective information. It is especially valuable when beginning a prospective survey, particularly for the study of immigration, to collect migration histories and data on important past events (employment, marriage and childbearing, education).

When there is an ongoing longitudinal survey, such as the PSID, with a highly qualified staff and a data dissemination program, it would be cheaper and more feasible to build on such a survey for additional longitudinal data on immigrants. For a major longitudinal survey of immigrants to be started, it may be cost-effective to consider building it onto a major ongoing longitudinal data collection program. But, as noted earlier, some existing longitudinal surveys do not offer an adequate representation of the ethnic and racial diversity of the U.S. population. It would cost considerably more to redesign an existing survey to include an adequate comparison group of the contemporary U.S. population, in addition to the costs of an immigrant subsample.

Discussion of current major longitudinal surveys illustrates two dilemmas faced by immigration researchers. First, the PSID now includes a Hispanic supplement but does not collect data on new immigrants. The study design does not recruit immigrants into its cohort data collection. A longitudinal survey of immigrants would require some ways to replenish the study with new entrants.

New immigrants might be added each year, or perhaps a special immigrant supplement of recent immigrants could be added every 3 to 5 years. Second, the Survey of Income and Program Participation (SIPP) currently recruits a new sample each year, following the study population for a 32-month period. In 1996, the Bureau of the Census is proposing to change the SIPP survey design and recruit a new and larger sample every 4 years, following the cohort for 4 years. SIPP, however, does not include a sufficiently large sample of immigrants for analysis. The SIPP survey design could oversample for some geographic areas or for foreign-born respondents, providing sufficient numbers of recent immigrants for separate analysis. Oversampling of recent immigrants in SIPP would provide valuable data, but it would also increase the survey complexity and cost.

This report has dealt with a number of improvements other than a new longitudinal survey of immigrants that would provide immigration researchers with better data. Although a longitudinal survey of immigrants would be extremely useful, workshop participants recognized that developing and funding such a survey would require a strong and committed coalition of academic and public policy researchers.

References

Anderson, Barbara A.
 *1992 Considerations in Longitudinal Research on Immigrants. Paper presented at the Work-
         shop on U.S. Immigration Statistics, National Research Council, Washington, D.C., Sep-
         tember 17-18.
Bean, Frank D.
 *1992 U.S. Immigration Trends and Policies: Recent Patterns and Emerging Contradictions.
         Paper presented at the Workshop on U.S. Immigration Statistics, National Research Coun-
         cil, Washington, D.C., September 17-18.
Bean, F.D., and M. Fix
  1992 The significance of recent immigration policy reforms in the United States. Pp. 41-55 in
         G. Freeman and J. Jupp, eds., *Nations of Immigrants: Australia, the United States, and
         International Migration.* Melbourne: Oxford University Press.
Bean, Frank D., Barry Edmonston, and Jeffrey S. Passel (eds.)
  1990 *Undocumented Migration to the United States: IRCA and the Experience of the 1980s.*
         Washington, D.C.: Urban Institute Press.
Bean, Frank D., Lindsay B. Lowell, and Lowell J. Taylor
  1988 Undocumented Mexican immigrants and the earnings of other workers in the United
         States. *Demography* February:35-52.
Bean, Frank D., Eduardo Telles, and Lindsay Lowell
  1987 Undocumented migration to the United States: perceptions and evidence. *Population
         and Development Review* 13:671-690.
Borjas, George J.
  1983 The substitutability of black, Hispanic, and white labor. *Economic Inquiry* 21(1):93-106.
  1986 The demographic determinants of the demand for black labor. Pp. 191-232 in Richard B.
         Freeman and Harry J. Holzer (eds.), *The Black Youth Employment Crisis.* Chicago: The
         University of Chicago Press.

─────────────

*Indicates a paper presented at the Workshop on U.S. Immigration Statistics, September 17-18,
1992.*

1990   *Friends or Strangers: The Impact of Immigrants on the U.S. Economy.* New York: Basic Books.

Borjas, George J., and Marta Tienda
1987   The economic consequences of immigration. *Science* 235(February):645-651.

Burnam, M.A., R.L. Hough, M. Karno, J.I. Escobar, and C.A. Telles
1987   Acculturation and lifetime prevalence of psychiatric disorders among Mexican Americans in Los Angeles. *Journal of Health and Social Behavior* 28:89-102.

Cherlin, Andrew
1988   *The Changing American Family and Public Policy.* Washington, D.C.: Urban Institute Press.

Chiswick, Barry R.
1977   Sons of immigrants: are they at an earnings disadvantage? *American Economic Review* 67(1):376-380.
1978   The effects of Americanization on the earnings of foreign-born men. *Journal of Political Economy* 86(5):897-921.
1982   The impact of immigration on the level and distribution of economic well-being. Pp. 289-313 in Barry R. Chiswick (ed.), *The Gateway: U.S. Immigration Issues and Policies.* Washington, D.C.: American Enterprise Institute.

Citro, Constance F., and Graham Kalton (eds.)
1993   *The Future of the Survey of Income and Program Participation.* Washington, D.C.: National Academy Press.

Eberstein, Isaac W.
1991   Race/Ethnicity and Infant Mortality. Paper presented at the annual meeting of the American Sociological Association, Cincinnati, Ohio, August.

Edmonston, Barry, and Jeffrey S. Passel
1994   *Immigration and Ethnicity: Integrating America's Newest Immigrants.* Washington, D.C.: Urban Institute Press.

Espenshade, Thomas J. (ed.)
1994   *A Stone's Throw from Ellis Island.* Lanham, Maryland: University Press of America.

Espenshade, Thomas J.
1992   Policy influences on undocumented migration to the United States. *Proceedings of the American Philosophical Society* 136 (2):188-207.

Fernandez-Kelly, M. Patricia
*1992   Labor Force Recomposition and Industrial Restructuring in Electronics: Implications for Free Trade. Paper presented at the Workshop on U.S. Immigration Statistics, National Research Council, Washington, D.C., September 17-18.

Greenwood, Michael J., and John M. McDowell
*1992   The Labor Market Consequences of U.S. Immigration. Paper presented at the Workshop on U.S. Immigration Statistics, National Research Council, Washington, D.C., September 17-18.

Guendelman, S., J.B. Gould, M. Hudes, and B. Eskenazi
1990   Generational differences in perinatal health among the Mexican American population: findings from HHANES 1982-84. *American Journal of Public Health* 80:61-65.

Hutchinson, E.P.
1956   *Immigrants and Their Children.* New York: John Wiley.
1958   Notes on the immigration statistics of the United States. *Journal of the American Statistical Association* 55:963-1025.

Jasso, Guillermina, and Mark R. Rosenzweig
1990   *The New Chosen People.* New York: Russell Sage Foundation.
*1992   U.S. Immigration and the Family. Paper presented at the Workshop on U.S. Immigration Statistics, National Research Council, Washington, D.C., September 17-18.

Karno, M., R.L. Hough, M.A. Burnam, J.I. Escobar, D.M. Timbers, F. Santana, and J.H. Boyd
  1987 Lifetime prevalence of specific psychiatric disorders among Mexican Americans and non-Hispanic whites in Los Angeles. *Archives of General Psychiatry* 44:695-701.
Kraly, Ellen Percy
  1979 Sources of data for the study of U.S. immigration. Pp. 34-54 in Stephen R. Couch and Roy Simon Bryce-Laporte (eds.), *Quantitative Data and Immigration Research.* Research Institute on Immigration and Ethnic Studies. Washington, D.C.: Smithsonian Institution.
Levine, Daniel B., Kenneth Hill, and Robert Warren (editors)
  1985 *Immigration Statistics: A Story of Neglect.* Washington, D.C.: National Academy Press.
Martin, Philip L. and J. Edward Taylor
  1991 Immigration reform and farm labor contracting in California. Pp. 239-262 in Michael Fix (ed.), *The Paper Curtain: Employer Sanctions' Implementation, Impact, and Reform.* Washington, D.C.: Urban Institute Press.
Masnick, George, and Mary Jo Bane
  1980 *The Nation's Families: 1960 - 1990.* Boston, Massachusetts: Auburn House.
Massey, Douglas S.
  1981 Dimensions of the new immigration to the United States and the prospects for assimilation. *Annual Review of Sociology* 7:57-85.
  1985 The settlement process among Mexican migrants to the United States: new methods and findings. Pp. 255-292 in Daniel B. Levine, Kenneth Hill, and Robert Warren (eds.), *Immigration Statistics: A Story of Neglect.* Washington, D.C.: National Academy Press.
Massey, Douglas, Rafael Alarcon, Jorge Durand, and Humberto Gonzalez
  1987 *Return to Aztlan: The Social Process of International Migration from Western Mexico.* Berkeley and Los Angeles: University of California Press.
Massey, Douglas S., and Luin Goldring
  *1992 Continuities in Transnational Migration: An Analysis of 13 Mexican Communities. Paper presented at the Workshop on U.S. Immigration Statistics, National Research Council, Washington, D.C., September 17-18.
Moscicki, E.K., B.Z. Locke, D.S. Rae, and J.H. Boyd
  1989 Depressive symptoms among Mexican Americans: the Hispanic health and nutrition examination survey. *American Journal of Epidemiology* 130:348-360.
North, David S.
  1995 *Soothing the Establishment: The Impact of Foreign-born Scientists and Engineers on America.* Lanham, MD: University Press of America.
Portes, Alejandro, and Robert L. Bach
  1985 *Latin Journey: Cuban and Mexican Immigrants in the United States.* Berkeley and Los Angeles: University of California Press.
Rumbaut, Rubén G.
  1990 *Immigrant Students in California Public Schools: A Summary of Current Knowledge.* CDS Report No. 11. Baltimore: Center for Research on Effective Schooling for Disadvantaged Students, The Johns Hopkins University.
  *1992 A Problem in Search of an Explanation: Some Research Questions on Assimilation and Immigrant Health, Mental Health, and Education. Paper presented at the Workshop on U.S. Immigration Statistics, National Research Council, Washington, D.C., September 17-18.
Rumbaut, Rubén G., and John R. Weeks
  1989 Infant health among Indochinese refugees: patterns of infant mortality, birthweight, and prenatal care in comparative perspective. *Research in the Sociology of Health Care* 8:137-196.

Schuck, Peter
1990 The great immigration debate. *The American Prospect* (Fall):100-118.

Smith, James P.
*1992 Labor Markets and Economic Assimilation of Hispanic Immigrants. Paper presented at the Workshop on U.S. Immigration Statistics, National Research Council, Washington, D.C., September 17-18.

Tienda, Marta
*1992 What We Don't Know Hurts Us: Data Needs and Research Priorities for Immigration and Income Maintenance Policy. Paper presented at the Workshop on U.S. Immigration Statistics, National Research Council, Washington, D.C., September 17-18.

Tomasi, S., and C.B. Keely
1975 *Whom Have We Welcomed?* New York: Center for Migration Studies.

U.S. Immigration and Naturalization Service
1992 *Statistical Yearbook of the Immigration and Naturalization Service.* Washington, D.C.: U.S. Government Printing Office.

Vega, William A., and Rubén G. Rumbaut
1991 Ethnic minorities and mental health. *Annual Review of Sociology* 17:251-383.

Warren, Robert, and Ellen Percy Kraly
1985 *The Elusive Exodus: Emigration from the United States.* Washington, D.C.: Population Reference Bureau.

Weeks, John R., and Rubén G. Rumbaut
1991 Infant mortality among ethnic immigrant groups. *Social Science and Medicine* 33 (3):327-334.

White, Michael J.
*1992 A Longitudinal Survey of Immigrants: Issues and Opportunities. Paper presented at the Workshop on U.S. Immigration Statistics, National Research Council, Washington, D.C., September 17-18.

Williams, R.L., N.J. Binkin, and E.J. Clingman
1986 Pregnancy outcomes among Spanish-surname women in California. *American Journal of Public Health* 76:387-391.

Yu, Elena
1982 The low mortality rate of Chinese infants: some plausible explanations. *Social Science and Medicine* 16(1982):253-265.

Appendix
Workshop on U.S. Immigration Statistics: An Assessment of Data Needs for Future Research

AGENDA

17-18 September 1992
Committee on National Statistics and Committee on Population
National Academy of Sciences

Green Building, Room 104
Georgetown Facility
2001 Wisconsin Avenue, N.W.
Washington, D.C.

Sponsored by
Immigration and Naturalization Service
and
National Institute for Child Health and Human Development

Thursday, 17 September

Introductions and opening remarks	Michael Teitelbaum, Chair
Commission on Behavioral and Social Sciences and Education	Suzanne Woolsey
Committee on National Statistics	Miron Straf
Committee on Population	Samuel Preston
Immigration and Naturalization Service (INS)	Gene McNary
National Institute for Child Health and Human Development (NICHD)	Wendy Baldwin
INS Data Programs and Future Needs	Edward J. Lynch
NICHD Research Purpose	Nancy Moss

Session 1   Immigration Trends: Magnitude and Characteristics
             (Rapporteur: Jeffrey Passel)
             Presenters   Michael Greenwood
                                                Frank Bean
             Panelists   Sherrie Kossoudji
                                                Karen Woodrow
                                                Discussion

Session 2   Assimilation and the Impact of Immigration on Health,
             Education, and Social Programs (Rapporteur: Steven Sandell)
             Presenters   Marta Tienda
                                                Rubén Rumbaut
             Panelists   Alejandro Portes
                                                W. Parker Frisbie
             Discussion

Session 3   Labor Force Issues (Rapporteur: Lindsay Lowell)
             Presenters   James P. Smith
                                                M. Patricia Fernandez-Kelly
             Panelists   Thomas Espenshade
                                                Robert Bach
             Discussion

Friday, 18 September

Session 4   Family and Social Networks (Rapporteur: Lisa Roney)
             Presenters ,   Douglas Massey
                                                Mark Rosenzweig and
                                                Guillermina Jasso
             Panelists   Bryan Roberts
                                                Mary Waters
             Discussion

Session 5   Data Needs for Measuring the Impact of Immigration
             Reports from Rapporteurs   Jeffrey Passel
                                                Lindsay Lowell
                                                Steven Sandell
                                                Lisa Roney
             Discussant   Robert Warren
             Discussion

Session 6   Design and Implementation of Longitudinal Studies
             Presenters   Barbara Anderson
                                                  Michael White
             Panelists   William Butz
                                                  Robert Gardner
             Discussion

Session 7   General Discussion of Where We Go From Here
             Discussion
             Concluding Remarks   Jeffery Evans
                                                  Edward Lynch

PAPERS PRESENTED AT THE WORKSHOP

Barbara A. Anderson, "Considerations in Longitudinal Research on
    Immigrants"
Frank D. Bean, "U.S. Immigration Trends and Policies: Recent Patterns and
    Emerging Contradictions"
M. Patricia Fernandez-Kelly, "Labor Force Recomposition and Industrial
    Restructuring in Electronics: Implications for Free Trade"
Michael J. Greenwood and John M. McDowell, "The Labor Market
    Consequences of U.S. Immigration"
Guillermina Jasso and Mark R. Rosenzweig, "U.S. Immigration and the
    Family"
Douglas S. Massey and Luin Goldring, "Continuities in Transnational
    Migration: An Analysis of 13 Mexican Communities"
Rubén G. Rumbaut, "A Problem in Search of an Explanation: Some Research
    Questions on Assimilation and Immigrant Health, Mental Health, and
    Education"
James P. Smith, "Labor Markets and Economic Assimilation of Hispanic
    Immigrants"
Marta Tienda, "What We Don't Know Hurts Us: Data Needs and Research
    Priorities for Immigration and Income Maintenance Policy"
Michael J. White, "A Longitudinal Survey of Immigrants: Issues and
    Opportunities"

WORKSHOP PARTICIPANTS

Barbara A. Anderson, Population Studies Center, University of Michigan

Robert L. Bach, Department of Sociology, State University of New York, Binghamton

Wendy H. Baldwin, National Institute for Child Health and Human Development

Frank D. Bean, Population Research Center, University of Texas, Austin

Cynthia Buckley, Department of Sociology, University of Texas, Austin

Greg Butler, Policy Development, U.S. Department of Justice

William P. Butz, Associate Director for Demographic Fields, U.S. Bureau of the Census

Karen Carver, National Institute for Child Health and Human Development

Julie DaVanzo, Economics and Statistics Department, The RAND Corporation

William Diaz, The Ford Foundation

Thomas Espenshade, Office of Population Research, Princeton University

V. Jeffery Evans, National Institute for Child Health and Human Development

M. Patricia Fernandez-Kelly, Institute for Policy Studies, Johns Hopkins University

W. Parker Frisbie, Population Research Center, University of Texas, Austin

Robert W. Gardner, Brunswick, Maine

Maria E. Gonzalez, Office of Information and Regulatory Affairs, U.S. Office of Management and Budget

Linda Gordon, Immigration and Naturalization Service

Steve Goss, Office of the Actuary, Social Security Administration

Michael J. Greenwood, Department of Economics, University of Colorado

Manuel Garcia y Griego, School of Social Sciences, University of California, Irvine

Linda Hardy, National Science Foundation

Michael Hoefer, Statistics Division, Immigration and Naturalization Service

Guillermina Jasso, Department of Sociology, New York University

Sherrie A. Kossoudji, Department of Economics, University of Michigan

Ellen P. Kraly, Department of Geography, Colgate University

Roger Kramer, U.S. Department of Labor

Eric Larson, Program Evaluation and Methodology Division, General Accounting Office

B. Lindsay Lowell, Immigration Policy and Research, U.S. Department of Labor

Edward J. Lynch, Office of Strategic Planning, Immigration and Naturalization Service

Douglas S. Massey, Population Research Center, NORC/University of Chicago

Gene McNary, Immigration and Naturalization Service

Leslie Megyeri, Subcommittee on International Law, Immigration, and
    Refugees, U.S. House of Representatives
Nancy Moss, National Institute for Child Health and Human Development
Jeffrey S. Passel, The Urban Institute
Alejandro Portes, Department of Sociology, Johns Hopkins University
Samuel H. Preston, Population Studies Center, University of Pennsylvania
Bryan Roberts, Population Research Center, University of Texas, Austin
J. Gregory Robinson, Population Division, U.S. Bureau of the Census
Lisa Roney, Immigration and Naturalization Service
Mark R. Rosenzweig, Department of Economics, University of Pennsylvania
Rubén G. Rumbaut, Department of Sociology, San Diego State University
Steven Sandell, The Urban Institute
Richard Schauffler, Department of Sociology, Johns Hopkins University
James P. Smith, Labor and Population Program, The RAND Corporation
Shirley Smith, Immigration Policy and Research, U.S. Department of Labor
Jay D. Teachman, Department of Sociology, University of Maryland
Michael S. Teitelbaum, Alfred P. Sloan Foundation
Marta Tienda, Population Studies Center, University of Chicago
Robert Valdez, The RAND Corporation
Stephanie Ventura, National Center for Health Statistics
Joyce Vialet, Library of Congress
Eric Wanner, Russell Sage Foundation
Robert Warren, Statistical Analysis Bureau, Immigration and Naturalization
    Service
Robert Warren, Department of Sociology, University of Wisconsin
Ruth Wasem, Library of Congress
Mary Waters, Department of Sociology, Harvard University
Michael J. White, Department of Sociology, Brown University
Karen Woodrow, Center for Social and Demographic Analysis, State
    University of New York, Albany
Christian Zlolniski, Department of Anthropology, University of California,
    Santa Barbara

National Research Council Staff

Michele L. Conrad, Committee on National Statistics
Barry Edmonston, Committee on National Statistics
Helen M. Lopez, Committee on National Statistics
Linda Martin, Committee on Population
Miron Straf, Committee on National Statistics
Suzanne H. Woolsey, Commission on Behavioral and Social Sciences and
    Education
Meyer Zitter, Committee on National Statistics